Paula Nelson's Guide to Getting Rich

Also by Paula Nelson

THE JOY OF MONEY
WHERE TO GET MONEY FOR EVERYTHING

PAULA NELSON'S GUIDE TO GETTING
RICH

PAULA NELSON

G. P. PUTNAM'S SONS / NEW YORK

G. P. Putnam's Sons
Publishers Since 1838
200 Madison Avenue
New York, NY 10016

Library of Congress Cataloging-in-Publication Data

Nelson, Paula, date.
Paula Nelson's Guide to getting rich.

1. Success in business.   2. Finance,
Personal.   3. Women in business.   I. Title.
II. Title: Guide to getting rich.
HF5386.N34   1985   650.1'2   85-9550
ISBN 0-399-13030-6

Printed in the United States of America
2   3   4   5   6   7   8   9   10

Acknowledgments

With every book there is a family of loving and devoted souls who make up the team: Barbara Friedman, Trish Glover, Patrice Gunn, Sterling Lord and Bob Wool.

There is also an even larger cheering section: Ruth Alben, Marjorie Powell Allen, Lilia Arguello, Miriam Bass, Janet Blair, Heleain Blum, Grey Boone, Bill Brangham, Jackie & Bert Briskin, Irma Finn Brosseau, Ann Brown, Sonny Brown, David Burns, Paddy Calistro, Denise Cavenaugh, Marilyn Nibleck Cockett, Charleen Cooper Cohen, Marty Cohen, Joy Colton, Ron Crawford, Fred Dobbs, Robert Dodds, Mary Donaghue, Bill Doty, Henry Ehrlich, Donald Epstein, Jim Fawcett, Valerie Franklin, Jerry Franks, David Glover, Leonard Goldberg, Elaine Taylor Gordon, Gigi Graveline, Peter Greenberg, John Greth, Nesta Greth, Scott Greth, Jo Hartley, Gail Hays, Dan Hillman, Sheri Hirst, Andrew Jaffee, Sandy Joseph, Susan Kasen, George Labovitz, Winnie Lethbridge, Bob & Pat Lindh, Duncan McMillian, Patrick McNee, Pat & John Martin, Alex Mass, Tom Mintz, Lise & Rich Moreno, Rose Nelson, Bill Newbern, Tim Nordin, Gina Osti, Nick Osti, Robert Page, Sheila Peters, Howard Portegais, Brigette Potter, Blanche Ross, Cary Ross, Bob Rothenberg, Tom Shell, Anne Steinbeck, Marian Shuster, Dawna Turner and all my friends and members of BPW.

To all of you, my love and thanks!

To
Sterling Lord

With Special Appreciation to:
Barbara Friedman
For her talent, humanity and dedication.

Contents

CHAPTER 1
Get Ready to Get Rich 13

CHAPTER 2
EO3: Economic Orbit of Opportunity 19

CHAPTER 3
STP: Spot It/Test It/Package It 47

CHAPTER 4
PTP: Put Yourself in a Position to Profit 75

CHAPTER 5
NCR: No Cash Required 99

CHAPTER 6
PAPA: Profitable Attitude/Profitable Action 117

CHAPTER 7
Risk Taking/Reward Getting 139

Contents

CHAPTER 8

PEP: Passion Equals Profit 163

CHAPTER 9

HALT: High Action/Low Talk 175

Appendix: The Business Plan 187

CHAPTER 1

Get Ready to Get Rich

You've hit the Economic Wall.

You have all the ingredients for success: You're bright, talented, hardworking, and ambitious, yet something isn't quite right. A closer look at your bank account tells the tale—financially you're merely treading water.

You may have the job you only dreamed about five years ago, good contacts, and enough responsibility for three people. Or you might be coming back to the career ranks after years of raising a family. Or perhaps you're somewhere in between, stalled on the middle management ladder, eyeing the top-paying spots just out of reach.

Whatever your situation, you've probably reached the same sobering conclusion: your paycheck is somehow never enough and you're wondering if it ever will be.

That's why I've written this book—to give you

my eight essential principles for making the transition from merely making a living, to making serious money.

During my nearly twenty years as a businesswoman, financial writer, lecturer, and consultant, I've learned that making serious money doesn't happen by accident. It doesn't happen through traditional thinking or traditional action, and it rarely comes about through a paycheck. I've also learned that while it isn't limited by age, position, education, or geography, serious moneymaking does require a mind-set all its own.

That mind-set is not taught on university campuses or in MBA programs, but is drawn from instinct and honed on the firing line of experience. Those two elements have served as my foundation in developing the eight principles in this book— principles that will give you the essential ingredients for making serious money.

These are the same principles that I used when launching my first company, Infonics, Inc., a fledgling garage operation that became a multimilliondollar electronics firm that in a brief three years became publicly traded and earned me my first serious money before the age of twenty-five.

They are the same principles that enabled me to launch four more million-dollar ventures and help dozens of others do the same. I've used them for years in my work with banks and top financial institutions as well as with Fortune 500 companies and their executives. And I use them to show my seminar and lecture audiences (and the people I work with in my consulting business) how to see and act upon financial opportunities all around them—opportunities they didn't even realize they had. As you'll see in the coming pages, my principles have helped even money novices achieve dramatic financial success—and they'll show you, too, how to start thinking and acting in terms of profit potential in all aspects of your financial life, beginning right where you are today.

PAULA NELSON'S
PRINCIPLES FOR MAKING SERIOUS MONEY

Principle 1—Economic Orbit of Opportunity

You have an Economic Orbit of Opportunity composed of all the factors that make your environment, experiences, and economic assets unique from everyone else's. That Economic Orbit is made up of the city in which you live, the publications you read, the people you know, the hobbies you enjoy. It includes your paycheck, retirement program, fringe-benefit package, credit rating, education, career, and special areas of expertise. Your Economic Orbit provides you with valuable insights into moneymaking opportunities *you probably don't even know you have,* and it also offers you untapped financial resources with which to pursue those opportunities. You'll see how others have applied this principle to their own lives—and how you can too.

Principle 2—Spot It/Test It/Package It

It doesn't do any good to have a great idea or spot a terrific opportunity unless you're able to take it past the conceptual stage. If you are creative and imaginative enough to spot a need in the marketplace, you owe it to yourself to carry your concept two steps further—to test the viability of the idea and then package it and take it to the marketplace. You'll learn how to translate ideas and investment opportunities into profit and meet a number of people who have done just that.

Principle 3—Put Yourself in a Position to Profit

The majority of people I meet are profit-blocked. No matter what they do, how hard they work, or how many hours they log on their time clock, the result is the same—a paycheck and nothing more! This principle will give you the four proven methods for establishing and then reaching your personal money goals. It will show you how to apply the concept of lateral moves and quantum leaps to create profit structures, as well as how to take the steps necessary to position yourself for serious moneymaking.

Principle 4—No Cash Required

Hundreds of my clients have marketed their inventions, purchased real estate, invested in the stock market, and set up their own companies—without investing even a penny of their own money! This principle will show you how it's done.

Principle 5—Profitable Attitude/Profitable Action

There is only one person who ultimately decides whether or not you're going to be a financial success: you. In order to make serious money, you must first believe in your own moneymaking potential. This principle will show you how to dissolve the money myths that are keeping you from reaching your goals and help you avoid the most common—and the most destructive—money games. I'll describe the actions and attitudes common to all money-makers and tell you how you can follow their example.

Principle 6—Risk Taking/Reward Getting

By examining the six components of every risk, you'll learn how to stop being crippled by the fear of taking financial chances. This principle will show you how to create your own Risk Environment Safety Net, and teach you to recognize your Risk Comfort Zone.

Principle 7—Passion Equals Profit

The moneymaking opportunities that will work best for you are those that inspire your enthusiasm and pique your interest. This principle will demonstrate how to tune in to your own investment personality by valuing your passions (hobbies, entertainment, favorite foods, etc.) and turning them into financial opportunities.

Principle 8—High Action/Low Talk

The foregoing seven principles mean nothing without the last—and perhaps most important—which stresses the crucial aspect of *active commitment* to the moneymaking process. In this chapter, I'll demonstrate how to take immediate action, no matter which avenue you choose to reach your financial goals.

By using these eight principles, you'll soon realize that your best moneymaking opportunities are probably within arm's reach of where you are right now. You'll learn how to refocus, reposition, repackage, and redirect your currently undervalued and underutilized talents, ideas, and expertise. And you'll do it all without sacrificing your career, your security, or your savings.

CHAPTER 2

EO3: Economic Orbit of Opportunity

If you're like most people, you probably equate financial success with big-money deals and Wall Street tycoons. You think serious money is something that happens to someone else, someplace else—but never to you. You're almost convinced that there is a secret "money success club" whose members all have the inside word on hot trends and moneymaking ideas.

The simple truth is that financial success is right there within your reach, no matter where you might happen to be. Time and time again, in my own experience and that of other serious moneymakers I have known, it's been proven to me that financial success grows out of a very special mindset—a way of looking at the world as a veritable cornucopia of potentially profitable opportunities.

That mind-set is crucial to your success in the

financial arena and, while some apply it almost by instinct, it can also be learned.

The experience of Susan Reynolds offers one of the best examples I've ever seen of someone who intuitively and profitably applied the principle of Economic Orbit of Opportunity to a moneymaking situation. She acted on her instincts and scored a financial coup.

Not long ago, over a cup of coffee, she told me her story.

"I had a very demanding job at the time, one that usually meant working late at the office each evening and stopping at a fast-food place on my way home for a takeout dinner," she said. "I started going to the local Kentucky Fried Chicken store several times a week to get my dinner-to-go. As the months went by, I noticed that the line to place an order was longer and longer each time. Obviously, a lot of other people were enjoying the chicken as much as I was.

"I decided to take a better look at what was going on to see if it could mean a moneymaking opportunity. I made an appointment with a stockbroker and asked him to tell me all about the company that owned Kentucky Fried Chicken and, in particular, whether it was publicly held, whether stock was offered to the public. I heard everything he had to say and asked him how much the stock cost.

"'Twenty-five dollars a share,' he told me.

"I bought all I could afford at the time, ten shares. As things turned out, I'd buy more later.

"He quickly executed the order and the stock began to move up almost immediately. The following week I got a call from my broker suggesting that I sell and take a nice profit.

"I told him I wasn't ready to sell yet, but that I'd let him know when I was. Two weeks later, I took a bonus check and turned it all into Kentucky Fried Chicken stock.

"Well, that broker didn't hear from me for a year. Then, one morning, I walked into his office and told him that I was ready to sell all my Kentucky Fried Chicken stock. He moved quickly, taking care of the transaction without so much as a comment. But, as I was about to leave his office, he couldn't resist any longer.

" 'Tell me something. Why did you choose today to sell?' he asked.

" 'For the past month or so, I've noticed that the lines were getting shorter and shorter when I placed my chicken order. And this week there was no line at all.'

"I stood up and walked out of the stock brokerage with my receipt for the stock sale in my handbag. I had made a tidy profit on my investment—and, sure enough, the stock started to take quite a dip soon after."

When you start to tune into your Economic Orbit of Opportunity, you'll find as Susan did that it provides you with insights into moneymaking opportunities you don't even realize you have. And you'll see that it also presents untapped financial resources with which to put those opportunities to work.

Made up of all the factors that comprise your environment, experiences, and economic assets, your Economic Orbit of Opportunity is as unique as your fingerprints. It has been shaped and influenced by your education, career, family and friends, hobbies and interests. It expands with each trip you take, publication you read, person you meet, and skill you acquire. It reflects the movies you see, the music you listen to, and, as Susan's story points out, even the foods you eat.

There are many ways in which to use your Economic Orbit of Opportunity. Stock market maneuvers, venture capital investments, product development and sales are all possible when you fully recognize—and then use—the information and expertise you have at your fingertips. You can become a consultant, write training manuals, start up a company offering a unique service, or use your knowledge in any one of a dozen other ways.

Take Carol Hoffman, a woman I met after a seminar I gave in Salt Lake City—a woman who, by every reasonable assessment, seemed to have little potential for dramatically turning her financial situation around, but who did just that after I showed her how to activate her own economic potential.

I had been comparing notes with the other speakers after the seminar when Carol walked up and introduced herself.

"Your lecture was terrific," she said. "Now I know what to do if I ever get a few thousand dollars together. But do you have any advice for people like me?"

"Tell me a little bit about yourself," I asked.

"I'm divorced. I have five kids. I don't have an extra dime, and I work for the local U.S. Post Office."

In traditional terms, she hadn't given me much to go on but, then again, I have never been a traditionalist when it comes to making money.

Seconds went by and I found my eyes fixed on the pin she was wearing on her lapel. It was the size of a stamp and appropriately said, "U.S. Postal Service." It reminded me of an article I had seen in *The Wall Street Journal* a few days earlier which told how corporations all across the country were wasting millions of dollars a year on quick, overnight mail services.

"Do you know anything about overnight mail service—you know, like Federal Express and Purolator?" I asked her.

"I should. I'm a manager at the Post Office. I deal with that sort of thing every day of the week."

"Could you tell business people about techniques they could use to cut the high cost of overnight mailing?"

"You bet I could," she said, and proceeded to tell me more than I could possibly want to know about the subject—facts, figures, and a number of different methods to cut costs and still speed mail from Point A to Point B.

It was late and I had to catch a plane back to Los Angeles. "Write down what you just said and send it to me," I suggested to Carol, handing her my business card. "I'll tell you how to take it from

23

there." I knew that from what she had told me, we had the basis for a proposal for a booklet and/or a computer program that would help corporations cut their postal expenditures—a proposal that could open the door to her financial independence by eventually generating royalties of from $15,000 to $20,000 a year.

At this writing, she is negotiating with two business publishers for the rights to her package.

The moral of that episode is not the product Carol is developing, but the process she started to follow of recognizing, valuing, and then tapping her own Economic Orbit of Opportunity. It shows what began to happen when she learned to take the emphasis off the classic assumptions about moneymaking and expand the focus to include her own very specific area of expertise.

The concept of Economic Orbit of Opportunity is also demonstrated by the success Karen Knight has enjoyed since she acquired a moneymaking mindset.

Karen, a whiz with numbers, was the accountant for a Nevada toy store when I first met her at a dinner party. I knew from our hostess that she was good at her job and enjoyed it tremendously. But Karen told me she was concerned about what she thought were poor management decisions by the store's owner—decisions she believed had placed the future of the operation in jeopardy.

"If only it were my store," she lamented, "I could really use what I know to make it successful. They're doing everything wrong, and that's why they're losing an average of three thousand dollars a month."

"If you think you could turn the business around, why don't you go out on a limb and try to do just that," I urged. "If the owner is losing as much money as you say he is, he might be delighted to find someone to take it off his hands. And you stand a chance of acquiring the store for a minimal cash outlay—or none at all."

When we met several days later at my office, I explained how she could offer to take over the store during the course of the next five years. It's common practice with the corporate giants, and it works the same for you or me. It's commonly called an earn-out deal. That's where you take over a business for no money now—but with the promise of a payout to the seller in three to five years when the company is making money.

I suggested that she write up a business plan (I'll tell you how in the Appendix) and told her to indicate in very specific terms how she would reverse the company's losses. Within a week, she had developed a plan that was simple yet effective—a plan that reflected her sound business sense as well as her firsthand knowledge of that particular retail operation.

Then she was ready for the next step—the presentation meeting. She invited the owner to lunch and presented her business plan, her suggestions for how she'd turn the company around, and her offer to take over the operation under the terms she and I had discussed. To Karen's amazement, the owner was not only interested in her suggestion, but was tremendously relieved, explaining that he had been looking for a way out of the venture for some time.

Karen took over the failing enterprise and went to work. Using the credit already established with distributors and suppliers, she ordered new stock. With $1,200 out of her own pocket, she painted the storefront and ordered a new sign. She began an advertising and public relations program stressing the huge variety of quality merchandise she had available.

The result? The store turned a solid profit for four consecutive years until she sold it a few months ago for $250,000.

Dana Edwards found a different avenue to serious money—but also one that took full advantage of her Economic Orbit of Opportunity. A manager with Chrysler Corporation, she attended a seminar I gave several years ago for members of the Detroit automobile industry. Like nearly everyone else in the audience, she was worried that she was working in the wrong industry at the wrong time in the wrong part of the country. She had every reason to feel that way: During her ten years with Chrysler, she had watched things go from bad to worse. The company's financial losses, the uncertainty about its future, and the general gloom and doom she felt all around her at the office were hardly the stuff that optimism is made of. But I saw her taking extensive notes during my presentation and, a year later, I received a letter from her that made my day.

"I took your advice," she wrote. "After looking at my Economic Orbit of Opportunity, I decided to focus my moneymaking activities on the thing I knew best—Chrysler Corporation—and I began to study the impact of the management changes that were being implemented by Lee Iacocca, who had taken over as Chairman of the Board. Those changes were both tangible and intangible—operations were being strengthened, belts were being tightened, and a new mood of optimism was emerging. I decided that if *we* were starting to feel good about the company and had a strong manager who was making wise decisions, it was certainly worth investing in what I felt would be a business reversal. I also knew that Chrysler stock was at an all-time low, selling at three dollars a share. How much worse could it get? I bought seven hundred shares—and yesterday I sold them at twenty-seven dollars! My situation certainly has changed. I'm happy to say that now I need any tips you might have on tax shelters!"

Dana's gamble worked because, even though the rest of the country was betting against Chrysler, she was right there in the trenches and sensed what was happening long before the "experts" caught on. And she trusted her perceptions enough to take what turned out to be extremely profitable action.

Peggy Martin is another woman who spotted a change in her Economic Orbit of Opportunity and profitably put that observation to work. She lives on a lovely, tree-lined street in Santa Monica, California. For years, the house next door to hers had been unoccupied, cared for by a handyman working for an absentee owner. One day, she noticed a group of people wandering around the house. She asked a few questions and learned that they were attorneys who were preparing to put the property up for probate sale.

She knew nothing about that kind of transaction, but recognized that acquiring the property next door would increase the value of her own land, as well as providing her with a lucrative rental. She decided to call her own attorney to find out how the whole thing was done—and whether the situation presented an opportunity worth pursuing. He explained that the probate process involves submittal of sealed bids and can sometimes result in acquisition of a valuable piece of real estate for a fraction of its market value.

Peggy retained him to do an appraisal search and handle the paperwork involved in the bidding process. When she finally submitted the bid, she was worried that her offer was far too low—approximately half the going price for a comparable house in that area. As it turned out, her only competitor was the postman, who had also seen the attorneys walking around the house. Her bid was $500 higher than his, and she walked away with the bargain of the decade, all because she observed something that was going on right under her nose and decided to check it out.

And, as Charlene Mosk learned several years ago, your Economic Orbit of Opportunity also involves situations that are a bit out of the ordinary, as well as those that happen in your own backyard. Through a friend, she attended a special movie preview for film critics. Knowing that they're generally quite jaded when it comes to cinema releases, she was surprised to hear the critics hooting and hollering for the space age heroes and villains flashing across the screen. The following day, she did some checking and found out that the movie *Star Wars* had been produced by 20th Century-Fox. She also learned that the company's stock was at an all-time low because of a string of box-office disasters. Trusting the sense of excitement she had felt at the screening, Charlene bought fifty shares of 20th Century-Fox Film stock at $20 per share. The last time I checked, it was selling at more than $70.

While few of us have the opportunity to attend a special film preview, Charlene's experience demonstrates how even going to a movie can become a moneymaking opportunity if you're prepared to see it that way.

Perhaps the most extraordinary example of this approach to financial success can be found in the story of Nolan Bushnell, founder of Atari Corporation, the maker of incredibly successful Pong and other computer games. While attending college at Brigham Young University, Nolan noticed that his classmates were spending all their time in the computer lab, playing games on the $40-million equipment. He thought how great it would be to produce and market similar games for wider distribution, but the computer's multimillion-dollar price tag made his idea just an ambitious daydream. He filed the idea away in the back of his mind and went on about his life.

Two years after Nolan graduated from college, he read about a major breakthrough in the computer industry—the invention of the microprocessor chip. He knew that it was the technological breakthrough that could make his daydream a reality.

He also realized that, while the computers no longer cost $40 million, they were still expensive enough to make the automated games he envisioned out of reach to a wide consumer audience. So, once again drawing upon his Economic Orbit of Opportunity, Nolan thought back on his summer jobs working at carnivals and recalled how enthused most people are about arcade games. Deciding to apply the same principle to computer games, he developed the first version of Pong, a coin-operated game he sold to restaurants and bars for $3,000 per unit. It was an instant hit and Nolan Bushnell was on the way to turning his $526 initial investment into the $36-million deal that eventually took place when he sold his company to Warner Communications Company.

I put my own EO3 powers of observation to work at my local supermarket, where I was looking in vain for Lean Cuisine frozen entrées. Traveling as I do about half the time, I invariably put on weight on the road and continually struggle to lose it at home. Searching through the frozen food area, I couldn't locate these low-calorie meals and lodged a complaint with the store manager.

"Miss Nelson," he said, shaking his head, "the problem is the tremendous demand for this product. I simply can't keep enough of it on hand."

At the check-out counter, I made a note on the back of my sales receipt: "Check out Lean Cuisine with stockbroker." A few follow-up calls provided me with the information that Lean Cuisine was manufactured by Stouffer's, which was owned by Nestlé. I didn't make any moves right then, but—like Nolan Bushnell—kept the information tucked away in the back of my mind.

Three months later I was at a conference which several executives from Carnation Corporation were also attending. I asked them what was new and exciting at their company, hardly expecting any revelations from this staid but successful firm. Their answer, however, surprised me.

"We're doing some interesting things in the diet area," they said. My ears perked up immediately. "We're testing something called The Diet Center here in Los Angeles. Are you familiar with Lean Cuisine? We're taking that concept and offering a total food package to the dieter."

"How do you think this will affect your stock?" I asked, trying to hide my excitement.

Suddenly they went mum. Clearly, stock information was not in the cards with this group.

The next morning I called my broker. "Jim, what do you know about Carnation?"

"Boring old Blue Chip company. Carnation has

been at thirty for the past five years. What more can I say?"

"Do you think it will drop below thirty? Could you have your analyst check it out and let me know what she says?"

He called back to tell me the company was holding steady on a status quo path.

"Jim, I'm thinking of buying some Carnation stock," I said.

"Why would you do a dumb thing like that?"

"Here's my thinking. As you know, I'm a diet nut. I like Lean Cuisine, Weight Watchers and all the other low-calorie prepackaged foods. Do you know who owns Weight Watchers? Heinz. They get you fat on one side, then show you how to take it off on the other," I explained with a certain sense of Catch-22 sarcasm. "I have a hunch that Carnation is moving in the same direction."

I bought a few shares at 30. My hunch turned out to be correct and Carnation recently closed at 55. It was a long road from talking to the supermarket manager about frozen dinners to buying stock in a food company with a very traditional image, but it just demonstrates how our EO3 is always presenting us with information we can act upon if we choose to do so.

Are you starting to see what I mean when I say that opportunities are waiting for you where you least expect them?

TAKING YOUR ECONOMIC ORBIT OF OPPORTUNITY INVENTORY

How can you make this theory work for you? Writing out an inventory of your Economic Orbit of Opportunity is the best move you can make to show yourself how many more opportunities you have than you imagine.

To do your own inventory, you'll need at least ten sheets of paper, just for starters. At the top of each, write one of the following category titles.

Career
Career Field
Family/Friends
Clubs/Associations
Geography
Food
Travel
Hobbies
Reading Material
Sports

Now you're ready to begin:

Career

Under the title "Career," write down exactly what you do for a living—manager, salesperson, writer, executive, bus driver, teacher, nurse, secretary, etc. If you work as a volunteer, write that down, and if you're a homemaker, you too should write down what you do. No matter what your line of work might be, think carefully for a minute or two and then list *all* the skills your career requires.

Include all the duties involved with what you do, the equipment you handle (whether it's a computer or a jackhammer), and the special expertise you have developed along the way. In order to chart a true picture of your Economic Orbit of Opportunity, you will need to list every area in which you have abilities that can eventually be tapped for your own benefit.

Next, write down the various types of information you've been exposed to through your career. Include the knowledge you have of trends, successes, failures, equipment development, acquisitions, and so on. You'll be amazed and impressed about how much information you already have.

As you proceed with this list, I believe you'll start to see what I mean when I say there are opportunities all around you. I'm reminded of Joanne Bates, a secretary who some years ago found one of the most exciting investment opportunities right under her nose—literally!

What were the three letters right in front of her as she sat at the typewriter for most of her working day? That's right—IBM. Joanne was a purchasing agent for an aerospace company when IBM introduced the revolutionary new "ball typewriter" in 1963. She noticed that her company had just bought twenty of the new machines—Selectrics—and she wondered if others were doing exactly the same thing. During a meeting with other corporate purchasing agents, she asked a few questions and learned that quite a few companies had also discovered the machine.

Joanne was not your typical Wall Street hotshot, so she spent some time tracking down a broker. She asked him to gather information on IBM—the annual report, quarterly reports, and any information from the brokerage analysts. She decided to buy as many shares of IBM as she could afford, which turned out to be a very shrewd move.

You might not want to invest in IBM, but I think this example shows you how your everyday expertise places opportunities right in front of you—opportunities that you have undoubtedly been ignoring because you didn't even realize they were there.

Speaking of secretaries and the opportunities their career-related expertise opens up to them, I'm reminded of Bette Graham, a very professional, dedicated secretary who knew there had to be a better way to remove errors from the typed page than the correcting tape and fluid that were then available. She experimented in her garage and developed a product, Liquid Paper, that made her an instantly successful entrepreneur.

Career Field

On this page of your inventory, describe the general field into which your specific career falls, such as the computer field, the nursing/health care field, the education field, the automotive industry. By carefully examining the broad field in which you work, you'll become aware of the gold mine of information at your disposal that you may choose to use as the basis of potential investments, entrepreneurial activities, or merely to store away as background for future actions.

Many people are intimidated by the Wall Street "experts," not realizing that they themselves are experts within their own fields. Think of it this way: You're right there in the trenches, you know what research is being done, which companies are hot, which mergers are likely to materialize, and where the most innovative new ideas are coming from in your area of expertise. You can take that information and use it as the basis for possible investments, or you might even decide to take the leap and develop your own solutions to the problems you see in your field. You already have information in your grasp that can lead you to a range of opportunities limited only by your own ambition.

For example, I recently gave a speech to a group of IBM executives in which I told them that the most profitable way for them to utilize their specific Economic Orbit of Opportunity was to examine the field in which they were working—the computer field, which is comprised of thousands of companies, ideas, breakthroughs, and developments, all representing potential investment opportunities. I suggested that the closer they look at trends in their own area of expertise, the better able they'll be to spot potential opportunities, whether they involve stock market investments, development of new techniques and/or pieces of equipment, or venture capital arrangements for new business endeavors.

IBM employees, for example, are more likely than most of us to have heard about a new company called Microsoft Corporation. In fact, they probably knew about the company long before its dramatic success story hit the mass media, and its founder, twenty-eight-year-old Bill Gates, ended up on the cover of *Time.* Whether they invest in Microsoft or just monitor the company's successes and innovations as part of their own research in preparation for developing a similar operation, people who work in the computer industry have valuable knowledge they can choose to use—but only if they are tuned into their Economic Orbit of Opportunity.

People in the computer field also saw the potential for computer graphics far sooner than the rest of us did. Those who valued their Economic Orbit of Opportunity acted upon their observation and checked out investment opportunities in the software and hardware computer graphics field. They sensed that this was going to be a good area for growth and used that awareness as a basis for their financial plans.

Do you see what I mean about how tapping your Economic Orbit of Opportunity becomes a building process?

Lest you take the last few examples as an indication that all the exciting opportunities are in the computer field, let's assume for a minute that your career is nursing and your career field is health care. This fact alone puts you in the position of knowing more about the pharmaceutical industry than most other people, and you're probably better informed about new surgical techniques and medical trends than any of the experts on Wall Street. You're undoubtedly well aware of the dramatic increases in health care costs and know first hand about a hot new trend called the Home Health Care Agency business, which is doing about $8 billion a year, with every expectation of being a $40 billion-a-year industry in the very near future.

Family/Friends

Yes, your family and friends are another very important aspect of your Economic Orbit of Opportunity. The expertise they possess can be a valuable source of information that you can share. On your inventory, list the careers of family members, their hobbies, sports they participate in, and any other special interests. You might even wish to sit down together to do a Family Economic Orbit of Opportunity Inventory. You'll find that the more people who are involved in filling out the inventory, the more interesting it becomes—and the more possibilities occur to you.

When I scan my own list of friends, I discover that it includes people who are experts in the arts, business, politics, publishing, computers, travel, medicine, finance, education, gardening, religion, cooking, psychiatry, sports, cars, zoos, jewels, horses, and so on. These people are invaluable sources of information; each represents years of expertise and each expands my own input level. Take a look at your circle of family and friends. I believe you'll be similarly impressed.

Clubs/Associations

Clubs and organizations can serve as great sources for all kinds of information, personal contacts, and possibilities for networking.

On this sheet of your inventory, list every organization you have been affiliated with. The Chamber of Commerce, Business and Professional Women, Girl Scouts U.S.A., YMCA, Lions Club, PTA, Rotary, Women in Business, Junior League, Soroptimists, League of Women Voters—write them all down and then add a few sentences about any special information or expertise you have picked up through your membership. The Chamber, for example, is a great source of information about areas of potential redevelopment and urban renewal.

Geography

Remember, no so-called expert knows as much about the area in which you live as you do. And the more you know about your own backyard, the more valuable that information becomes. On this page, list not only the city and state in which you live, but also the area of town and the region of the country you call home.

Now you're ready to start acquiring information within this framework. Find out who the largest employers in your area are and then begin to monitor their activities. Determine which industries form the backbone of your local economy and then read all you can about what's going on in those industries.

Let's take Seattle, for example. The largest employer in the city is the Boeing Corporation, and monitoring the business health of Boeing gives you a fairly accurate picture of what is happening in the Pacific Northwest in terms of economic growth. When Boeing is booming, not only is the Seattle economy booming, but the aerospace, aircraft, and military spending areas are thriving as well.

Seattle has also been the home ground for many exciting business ventures, including Microsoft, which I mentioned earlier. Few people other than Seattle residents and computer buffs knew anything about that company until just recently when it became a media darling. But those in Seattle who tapped their Economic Orbit of Opportunity took this observation through the process of Spot It/Test It/Package It—which you'll learn about in the next chapter—and were prepared to knowledgeably monitor Microsoft's activities and invest in the company when it went public.

Of course, your observations don't have to be on the level of a Boeing or a Microsoft. Take David's Cookies. People who live in New York knew about these exceptional treats long before the rest of the country and therefore had an investment advantage. Those in Salt Lake City had a head start on gathering information about another dynamic new company, Mrs. Field's Cookies.

And people in Baltimore, Maryland; St. Louis, Missouri, and Toledo, Ohio, have had a great opportunity to watch the impact of a redevelopment genius by the name of James Rouse, who has taken decaying urban areas and turned them into attractive, dynamic, profitable centers of economic activity. His knack for rejuvenating decrepit waterfront areas has revitalized entire areas of the cities in which he has been involved.

For those who are in tune to this kind of thing, the arrival of Rouse on the scene means that there will be new development in a previously blighted area, that property values will soar, and that the city itself is going to enjoy an infusion of new economic activity.

It's all based on what I call the Proximity Theory—the closer you are to something, the more you're likely to know about what's going on and the better able you'll be to get into situations that present sound opportunities.

Food

On this page of your inventory list all of your favorite foods and beverages, as well as your favorite restaurants. I've already told you about how my enjoyment of Lean Cuisine products indirectly led me to a tidy profit on an investment. You can do the same thing.

When you see a product that people seem unable to stay away from, get in the habit of checking to see if the company is publicly owned and therefore offers an opportunity for investment. Or if you have a special recipe that people clamor for, consider doing more than just including it in a charity cookbook. Investigate the possibility of submitting it to a manufacturer for licensing or, like a friend of mine who came up with the predecessor for the Celestial Seasonings Company, you might even market the product yourself.

Travel

Travel offers a virtual gold mine of information that can be brought into your Economic Orbit of Opportunity. It can also introduce you to people with experiences and backgrounds far different from your own, and this, too, serves to broaden your Economic Orbit of Opportunity.

Several years ago, I was vacationing in India and

noticed some fascinating papier-mâché boxes the likes of which I had never seen in the United States. I talked to the local distributor to check out the prices and investigate the possibility of importing the items. As it turned out, I decided not to go ahead with the endeavor, but passed the information on to a friend who owns a small boutique. She tells me she has made quite a profit on the boxes during the past few years.

Hobbies

List all the activities you are interested in: landscape gardening, painting, reading, sewing, whatever. Whether you're a stereo enthusiast or a Heathkit fan, your interest will make you aware of trends and companies to take a closer look at.

For example, crafts are a hobby area, but they're also one of the hotter trends in the retail field. As John Naisbitt points out in his book *Megatrends*, the crafts business is booming because the more we are surrounded by high technology in the work world and the marketplace, the more we crave the personal touch in things that are close to us.

Since crafts are currently a multibillion-dollar industry, you might want to consider marketing your craft items—or investing in a craft-oriented company.

Reading Material

Make a list of all the periodicals and publications you read on a regular or even an occasional basis. My own inventory in this particular area lists the approximately one hundred publications I scan every month for information I think might eventually prove profitable. I check *The Wall Street Journal, The New York Times, The Los Angeles Times, The San Jose Mercury News* (in order to keep up on what's going on in Silicon Valley), John Naisbitt's *Trend Report, Ms., Business Week, Vogue, Harper's Bazaar, Money* magazine, *The Financial Times* of London, *Barron's, Newsweek, Time, People, Fortune,* and three different newsletters—and that's just for starters. (Notice that not all of the publications I read are in the financial area. That's because I don't scan for financial information per se; I look for information that *leads* to financial decisions.)

Reading is the cheapest, quickest way to become an expert on virtually any subject you might be interested in. By investing a few dollars at the bookstore or a few hours at the local library, you can dramatically expand your Economic Orbit of Opportunity on any given subject. You'll find that your confidence will increase and your ability to spot opportunities will be enhanced.

Sports

List any sports that you are involved in: Jazzercize, aerobics, jogging, tennis, soccer, racquetball, and so on. A good example of someone who took a sport and converted it into a moneymaking proposition is Jane Fonda, who turned her own personal need for exercise into a book that became the basis for the entire "Jane Fonda industry."

Dodie Williams of Salt Lake City is another who converted her sports expertise into a moneymaking venture. An enthusiastic tennis player who was annoyed with the way her racquet head scraped on the ground when she was picking up wayward balls, she came up with a small, inexpensive ($1.95) invention that wrapped around and protected the head itself. Once again, you can see how someone tapped her Economic Orbit of Opportunity by seeing a solution to a problem based in her own range of experience.

Now that you've learned to see opportunities all around you, you've got the most crucial lesson in this book under your belt. Next comes the process of how to evaluate and act upon what you've seen— Spot It/Test It/Package It.

CHAPTER 3

STP: Spot It/Test It/ Package It

Moneymaking opportunities are all around you, but opportunities alone do not a profit make. My principle of Spot It/Test It/Package It will give you the process to take any opportunity—a product, a service, or an investment—from the conceptual stage to profitable action.

The process is simple: You spot an opportunity you'd like to pursue, you plan and test a course of action, and then you package—or act upon—the results. "Packaging" doesn't always mean producing and distributing an actual product—the process can also apply to purchasing a stock, investing in a venture capital situation, buying or forming a new company, investing in a real estate partnership, developing a new service, or any one of a number of other options, as Pat Nicholson recently discovered.

Pat is a hospital administrator and one of the

most charming and gracious hostesses I know. She entertains frequently, and the big hit at her parties is her food, most of which is based on family recipes. Particularly popular is a sweet mustard she serves with cheese and crackers. At a get-together not long ago, I complimented her on the mustard and asked where she bought it. "I don't buy it," she said. "I make it once a month."

I was surprised that anything so delicious hadn't already found its way to the shelves of my local market. With my typically entrepreneurial mindset, I asked if she'd be interested in a business venture based upon her recipe.

"I've thought of it, but I don't know where to begin," she said. "Besides, how am I going to find time to mix huge batches of mustard and label thousands of jars?"

Pat was struck with a common misconception about turning ideas or products into profit—that you have to do everything yourself.

I explained that there are any number of ways to make a profit from something you create, whether that creation is a product, a service, or an idea. You can produce it yourself, you can distribute it, you can sell the idea, you can go into partnership, or you can enter into a licensing agreement with someone willing to give you a percentage of their profit in return for the rights to use your concept.

I outlined a plan for Pat that could easily be set in motion in as little as fifteen to twenty hours of her time. At my urging, she tested market reaction to her mustard by taking samples to her local gourmet food store, where she met with a quick and enthusiastic reception from the store manager. He loved the taste of the sweet mustard and placed an order for twenty-four jars. After a similar reaction at three more stores during the next few weeks, I showed Pat how to use those orders as the basis for a licensing agreement that would net her a tidy 10 percent royalty fee for every jar of mustard sold.

She contacted several food distributors and, after a few meetings, found one that recognized the sales potential of the condiment and agreed to the terms of the deal. Based upon their sales projections, Pat expects to receive licensing fees of approximately $17,000 a year.

I particularly like that story because it clearly demonstrates that even after you spot an opportunity and develop a plan of action, there are many different ways to package the results. It also shows the importance of testing your concept, because no matter how great your idea might be, you won't stand a chance of making it work profitably unless you can come up with the right answers to the following questions:

- Can you do what you say you're going to do?
- Can you make a profit doing it?
- Will the market like your idea?

The only way to answer those questions is by taking your concept through the following four steps:

1. Create a prototype.
2. Draft a business plan.
3. Take your idea to the marketplace and try to get an order.
4. Package it.

Step 1: Create a Prototype

Have you ever tried to describe the color blue? It's just as difficult to adequately describe a new product to bankers, distributors, and potential customers unless they have something tangible they can see, touch, try, and react to. That's why you need to develop a sample that clearly demonstrates the value and uniqueness of your concept.

The same holds true for an intangible product or a service. In this case, the sample can be a brochure discussing the service, highlighting your capabilities, and describing your facilities and previous successes. The important thing is to come up with something visual—something you can actually put in the hands of prospective customers, investors, and distributors to indicate that your concept is more than just another interesting idea.

Step 2: Draft an Initial Business Plan

It needn't be fancy or elaborate at first, but a business plan is a must. It forces you to think through the practical and financial aspects of your idea, which is something many entrepreneurs would rather not take the time to do. The trouble with the entrepreneurial "fly-by-the-seat-of-your-pants" method of doing business is that you're really flying blind until you do a five-minute business plan. Your plan can be simple, focusing on the costs involved in offering your product or service and the market potential at that price. (See the Appendix for a detailed description of how to do a business plan.)

Step 3: Take Your Idea to the Marketplace (Show Up/Show Off)

This step provides the acid test of a new idea. My advice is to take your prototype directly to the largest convention you can find that deals directly with the field to which your concept applies. Going to a convention allows you to survey all aspects of the market and get the very important "feel" of what's going on. By "walking the show," you can learn more than you would in a dozen meetings or twenty telephone calls. Think of it this way: Where else will you be able to find hundreds of possible buyers, distributors, and backers in one place?

There is a valid concern about conventions, however, and that is, "How can I protect my idea at an open forum like that? How can I prevent others from knocking off or copying my concept?"

I admit that it's a double-edged sword. But think of it this way: You can take your concept to a convention and risk getting copied or you can decide not to show it at all and risk never getting the product or service to the market. My advice is to try to protect yourself as best you can. If your idea can be patented or copyrighted, you should definitely meet with a patent attorney to find out how to go about registering it. Your attorney can also draft a standard disclosure letter, which states that yours is a proprietary idea or product that you originated. Before showing your concept to a potential backer or distributor, you ask for a signature on a copy of the letter, which then serves as their agreement not to copy or duplicate your concept without your involvement.

If you're like most entrepreneurs, you probably have good instincts when it comes to people. Use them and be cautious without being paranoid. Or, as one inventor friend of mine put it, "Avoid people with cameras."

Step 4: Package It

Getting an order is the final stage in testing an idea for a product or service. If someone is willing to pay for what you're selling, you're in business. You'll still need to go through the production and/or licensing process, but you will have discovered that your idea works and that there is a demand in the marketplace for what you have to offer.

Several years back, an investment group came to me with an idea for a small viewer for Kodak 110 slides. Their plan was to develop a costly mold to mass-produce the plastic viewers, which they planned to sell for $9.95 each. I suggested that they make a prototype first and use it to secure orders, saving them the cost of the $35,000 mold if the item didn't strike a chord in the marketplace. Once they developed the sample, they followed my advice and took it to the largest distributor of photographic supplies in New York. They were delighted when the distributor wanted to place an order for 10,000 units—but not when he said he would only pay $2.50 each wholesale, since he didn't believe his customers would pay more than $4.95 retail for the item. Even though my clients wanted to try and fill the order, I convinced them they simply couldn't produce the viewer for less than $3 each, which meant they'd be losing 50 cents on each sale.

In my consulting work, I find that approximately half of my clients develop products for which the manufacturing costs are too high to permit profitable production and distribution. Like the investment group that saved $35,000 by waiting for orders before they went ahead with the expensive mold, they find that the process of taking a prototype to the marketplace saves them from getting involved in a venture with no future—and no payoff.

A story closer to home involves an experience I had with my first company, Infonics, which manufactured reel-to-reel audiotape duplication equipment. Like most manufacturers, we regularly attended the various industry trade shows held across the country, where we exhibited our latest products and checked out the other new developments in the field. At the 1967 National Audio Visual Association Convention in Atlantic City, it was obvious to my partner and me that the 3M Company had unveiled one of the most exciting new products we had seen—the audiocassette.

My partner, who had the advantage of fifteen years in the audioelectronics field, made the profitable observation that if the new tape format caught on, there would be a tremendous need for a process to make high-speed copies of materials recorded on those cassettes. And so began our move into what was then the new frontier of audiocassettes—a frontier in which all the experts told us that what we envisioned couldn't be done. But having spotted the potential need in the marketplace, we set about going through the four steps of developing and testing the new product we had in mind.

To make a one-year research and development story short, we produced and tested a prototype of a new tape-duplicating machine which we unveiled at the same convention the following year. The result of our efforts was $250,000 in sales during the three-day convention, as well as a two-and-a-half-year jump on our competitors with millions of dollars in orders. It was this jump that allowed our sales to multiply dramatically within a very short period of time, resulting in a public offering of our stock in 1969.

Development of a prototype allows you to discover whether your idea is workable, whether the product will be priced realistically, and whether it can be profitably produced and distributed.

For example, Gloria Mitchell, a college art teacher, already had her prototype when we met following an autographing session with my most recent book at a Cincinnati department store.

"I heard you interviewed on the radio this morning, and decided to come down here to see if you could tell me how to make some money with these," she said, as she showed me twelve lovely pen and ink drawings of local Cincinnati scenes. I was very impressed with her talent and told her so.

"You have the basis for a stunning line of note cards," I said. "Take the elevator up to the buying department right now and find the person who buys stationery items for the store. Ask his or her opinion of the idea, and ask for the name of the stationery sales-representative who covers this area."

I explained that once she had an order for the note cards, there would be more than one printer in town who'd be happy to produce them for a percentage of the order. (In Chapter 5, NCR: No Cash Required, you'll learn how to put together similar arrangements to get your product developed with little or no cash outlay on your part.)

I recently received a note from Gloria—on one of her note cards. She told me that she now travels from city to city, producing pen and ink drawings which her printing partner manufactures and the sales representative distributes.

Sharon Corr and her husband, Robert, were running a Chicago health food store eight years ago when they noticed the popularity of any product made with trendy but expensive ginseng. Deciding to try to come up with a new product to capitalize on this trend, they pored over old recipes and records until they discovered a dated formula that served as the basis for a soft drink–like beverage they developed called Ginseng Rush. They tested their product by taking it to industry trade fairs, where they received orders for thousands of cases. Their company, Corr's Natural Beverages, is now in the multimillion-dollar sales range.

Fred Dobbs, a long-time friend and business associate, developed, tested, and packaged an innovative audiocassette storage system that has saved his clients millions of dollars in warehousing fees. Fred owns a Dallas-based electronics firm that produces the audiocassettes used by a number of Texas insurance companies to record their claim reports. Since those reports have to be kept on file for a period of several years, the companies needed thousands of square feet of warehouse space to store them. Fred designed a cassette that popped open, allowing the magnetic tape to be removed and slipped into a small, envelope-like container, which could be stored in one-third the space of average cassettes. Fred secured a patent on his design, and is now the sole provider of the tapes to insurance companies all across the country.

Another of my clients is a doll house collector who decided to produce and market her own line of the diminutive houses. She developed prototypes in various architectural styles and then took her samples around to various meetings of collectors. The other collectors loved her houses, but found the $500 to $1,000 price tags far too steep to consider. I suggested that she could cut her labor costs by selling the houses in kit form, which would dramatically reduce the retail price. She is now offering her kits through toy stores, mail order, and do-it-yourself home parties.

HOW TO SPOT IT/TEST IT/PACKAGE IT WHEN THE OPPORTUNITY IS AN INVESTMENT

Once you spot an investment opportunity that intrigues you, the following test will help you to decide whether or not to pursue it.

Later in this section, I'll tell you how to evaluate various types of investments—the stock market, real estate, franchises, arts, and so on—but first, here is an Investment Test you can apply to any opportunity you're considering. The test will help you determine the soundness of a particular investment and whether it's the right one for you.

INVESTMENT TEST

1. What Are Your Reasons for Considering This Particular Investment?

Wise investing requires a careful matchup between the investor and the investment vehicle. Focusing on your reason for choosing a vehicle will help you ensure a good match. For instance, if your investment goal is to create a tax shelter, then you'd best choose real estate or research and development deals that are specifically designed as tax shelters, even though you might be interested in stocks and silver.

2. What Is the Track Record of the Investment and the Investment Group?

Whether you're dealing with a real estate syndicator or buying a new stock issue, it's essential that you know as much as possible about the vehicle and the people involved. To find out about the investment group, check with the Better Business Bureau, your local Chamber of Commerce, the corporation commissioner in your state, or the Federal Securities and Exchange Commission in Washington, D.C. Check, too, to see how long the group has been in business and ask your banker and CPA about the group's reputation. People in the financial community belong to an informal "club" and usually know—or know about—each other. Make a few inquiries. If your own expertise in a certain area is limited, by all means hire an expert to deliver an opinion on the deal. This may cost $100 or more, but it is better to seek professional advice now than later.

I also believe in taking the direct route and asking the group itself for information, including details about previous deals they've been involved in and their success on those deals. If your questions seem to make them nervous, then you're dealing with the wrong people. Remember, quality investment groups have nothing to hide—and successful people are proud of their successes.

3. What Are the Risks Involved in the Investment?

"What's the worst thing that can happen to me if I get involved in this deal?" That's the question that every prudent, smart, successful investor asks herself when confronted with an investment opportunity. You, too, need to determine your downside risk in each situation. For example, if you're thinking about buying a stock, your downside risk might be losing the entire amount you've invested. Are you willing to take that risk in order possibly to make a lot of money? Or would you be better off with a less chancy investment at this point in your life?

Take the story of Dana Edwards, who invested in Chrysler. Even though Chrysler was not on any brokerage "buy" lists, Dana made the decision to invest based upon (1) her observations of her Economic Orbit of Opportunity and (2) her analysis of a "worst-case" scenario, including finding out what would happen if Chrysler went bankrupt and was forced to liquidate. Her broker told her that under those circumstances the liquidation, or book value, of the stock would be $5 per share, which is still $2 over the price she'd be paying if she decided to buy it. In other words, even in the worst case of

Chrysler's going bankrupt, she'd make $2 per share on her investment! She couldn't lose. *Good deals are rarely that obvious.*

Another key question is "Do I have a way to limit my potential losses on this investment?" With stocks, you can limit your risk by placing a sell order on your holdings, which directs your broker to sell immediately when the stock's value falls below a certain level.

4. Can You Liquidate the Investment?

It's fairly easy to resell stocks, commodities, and bonds, but the waters get murky when you start talking about other types of investment. How easy would it be to get out of the investment you're considering if you decide to do so? Does it involve something that is easily salable? Can you choose to sell your share of the investment to partners?

In real estate partnerships, for example, you need to know what arrangements govern the sale of your interest in the property. Will the general partners buy back your portion if you decide to liquidate? Is there a "right of first refusal" arrangement giving the other partners the right to buy your interest before it is offered to an outside party, or can you sell on the open market? What is the resale market for the partnerships in your area?

5. How Do You Feel About the Opportunity?

This is the most important aspect of your decision about an investment. My advice is simple: Don't do it if you have any unanswered questions or negative feelings about the deal. There are literally hundreds of thousands of other moneymaking opportunities to choose from, so why go into something that doesn't feel comfortable enough to let you sleep at night?

And always remember: If an investment deal sounds too good to be true, it probably is.

Keeping those general investment criteria in mind, you can apply the following test process to specific investment vehicles:

HOW TO SPOT IT/TEST IT/PACKAGE IT WHEN THE INVESTMENT IS A STOCK

1. Check Out the Performance History of the Stock

Ask your broker for the stock's highs and lows—the highest and lowest prices it has sold for—as well as its current price. Also ask about its price/earnings, or P/E, ratio, which is a comparison between the price of a stock and the actual earnings of the company.

An average ratio is 10:1, while ratios in the range of 2:1 are very low and indicate an interesting opportunity. Ratios of 30:1 or more, on the other hand, are exceptionally high and evidence of a very high risk situation, since they show that people believe in the stock at a level that is far beyond what is warranted by the company's actual performance.

A good example of a high P/E ratio is a company called Genentech, a leader in the genetic sciences field that manufactures artificial plasma. When the company's stock went public several years back, its P/E ratio was 50:1. Investors were buying it up on the basis of little other than their assumption that it would be a huge financial success at some time in the future. They were willing to take a chance on that assumption, even though Genentech was in a loss position with millions of dollars invested in research and *not one penny of earnings.*

If you see a stock with an extremely high P/E level, let that be a warning it's a high-risk situation—one that only the very sophisticated investor should touch.

2. Find Out the Stock Analyst's Recommendation

Full-service brokerage houses such as Shearson Lehman/American Express, Merrill Lynch, and Dean Witter have entire departments of stock analysts who spend their time tracking specific stocks and securities. They talk regularly with key company officers, follow the company's ups and downs, and develop recommendations on stocks indicating their prognosis for future earnings. Any negative information about the company is also indicated in the analyst's report, which is available to the brokerage's clients.

3. Be Aware of the Risk Level Associated With Each Type of Stock

Stocks fall into three categories: high risk, medium risk, and low to zero risk. Examples of high risks are any and all new issues—that is, stocks that have no history because they're being offered to the public for the first time. Stocks are always accompanied by a prospectus which, in the case of new issues, usually includes a caution statement about the pitfalls of the stock. Only foolish investors ignore those warnings. Don't make that mistake unless you're so sold on the company that you are willing to accept the associated risks of buying the stock.

I once invested in a new issue that went from $20 a share on February 1 to 1/2 point (50 cents) a share on May 1. I ended up with a tidy tax-loss carry forward. I had expected a tidy profit!

The difference between growth stocks and Blue Chips is that all profits in growth stocks are placed back into the company rather than paying stockholders a dividend. The rationale is that you will make more on the increased value of the stock price.

And low to zero risks are the solid Blue Chips like IBM, General Motors, and ITT. While they rarely offer you colossal profits, they rarely keep you awake at night either.

HOW TO SPOT IT/TEST IT/PACKAGE IT
WHEN THE INVESTMENT IS REAL ESTATE

When considering a residential, commercial, or industrial real estate investment, a copy of the appraisal on the property will give you valuable background information to use in your evaluation. Some additional questions to consider include the following:

1. What is the asking price of the property?
2. Is that price firm or is it negotiable?
3. What are the prices of comparable properties in the immediate area?
4. How long has the property been on the market?
5. What is the resale climate in that vicinity? Have properties glutted the market or are they selling briskly? A glutted market is often a sign of a problem such as economic depression in the area. Find out the reason for the glut. If there are indications that it might be temporary, you might consider the purchase to be a qualified risk. If the situation looks irreversible, the investment

would probably turn out to be one to consider only at fire-sale terms.

6. If you're considering income property, you need to check out the details on the existing leases, rents, and payment records of the tenants. Ask to see the rental records and have them reviewed by your accountant.

7. What has the appreciation rate in the area been? Many areas are known for their high appreciation rates. You can check this fact with the broker you're dealing with.

8. Are the brokerage fees fixed or negotiable?

9. What type of financing is available on the property? The local savings and loan will have a history of the property and information on whether or not they will lend on it. Get loan rates from three to six mortgage lenders. Then check to see about the availability of nontraditional financing from the seller, such as an assumed second mortgage, a "wraparound" mortgage, assumption of the existing mortgage, and so on. Also check to see if the property qualifies for any tax advantages, such as the tax credits available on renovations of old buildings.

HOW TO SPOT IT/TEST IT/PACKAGE IT
WHEN THE INVESTMENT IS IN THE ARTS

The test process for an investment opportunity in the arts involves a determination of the authenticity and established market value of the work. Museums and the major auction houses, such as Sotheby's and Christie's, are the best sources for validating authenticity of art pieces. There is usually a fee for this service.

If you're thinking of buying a piece from a private party or collection, I strongly advise taking the piece to a major art/auction house in your area to get a sense of its potential resale value—and the house's willingness to handle such a sale.

Questions to consider when evaluating an art investment include:

1. What is the estimated value of the piece?
2. How rare is it?
3. What is the value of record—that is, what is the last sale price based on established catalogue value?
4. Where is the resale market for the piece? Works of art are so often moved from one area of the world to another in order to take advantage of shifts in demand. Find out if

66

the piece you're considering is highly valued in your area or in another spot.

HOW TO SPOT IT/TEST IT/PACKAGE IT WHEN THE INVESTMENT IS A BUSINESS

The most important considerations in evaluating a business are the worth of the company and the terms of the deal. By going through the following questions, you'll have a clearer idea of both.

1. What Are You Really Buying?

This question isn't as silly as it seems. You need to determine what the company's strongest assets are—and then be certain that those assets are what you'll be getting if you buy the business. For example, if a company's success is a reflection of the personality and charisma of its current owner, be prepared for a downturn under new management.

A major East Coast publishing corporation learned that lesson when it purchased a Los Angeles sales training firm not long ago. The training firm's president sold his shares and left the company within a year of the purchase, and the company's sales dropped in half without his very personal style of leadership.

Another investment group purchased an electronics company, thinking that its assets were the technical innovations it had regularly produced. The investors filled up three moving trucks with inventory, drawings, bookkeeping records, office furniture, and equipment and moved the operation across the country. The business failed because they hadn't realized that it was the company's middle management who had been responsible for the steady stream of moneymaking ideas—and who had provided the front-line leadership that stimulated and encouraged innovation.

2. What Is the Company's Position in Its Field?

What percentage of its market does the company "own"? Is it a leader or one of the pack? What will it take for you to maintain that market position—or to expand upon it? For example, IBM controls more than 50 percent of the market for most of the product areas it's in. A new company going up against IBM can never hope to win a large share of that market, but it can discover a market niche that IBM may have neglected. By focusing on a smaller segment of the market, the new firm can gain a strong market position in an area that the industry giant may have considered too small to be concerned with. That niche might generate very strong sales and equally healthy profits.

3. What Is the Company's Financial Position?

Is the company that rarest of all rare finds—a financially secure operation? Or is it like most businesses, needing cash for operations and/or expansion? Keep one fact in mind—a company is usually up for sale because of something to do with finances.

4. What Is the Reason for the Sale of the Company?

As I just said, the reason is usually related to finances, but there are exceptions—and you can sometimes make a wise purchase if you're aware of them.

I was once involved in a deal in which the initial asking price for a distributorship was $750,000. As the negotiations proceeded, my associates and I began to sense that the two owners of the company seemed to have a great deal of animosity for each other. We decided to offer them $250,000 in cash to see what they would do. As it turned out, they had such a deep and noisy hatred for each other, they both wanted out—even at a loss. They took our offer—saving us $500,000.

5. What Are the Terms of the Deal?

In nearly every deal the sellers will initially present the terms as inflexible. In order to make a smart purchase, however, you'll need to determine the degree of leeway you can introduce to the negotiations. The clue is to find out as much as you can about the owners' motivations for selling. Is there a personality clash such as the one I just mentioned? Are the owners facing a divorce? Planning to move to another area? Hoping to back a new venture with the capital they'll realize from the sale of this business? If the sellers aren't in any rush to get rid of the business, they clearly have the upper hand in the deal.

6. Does the Company Have Financeable Assets That Can Be Used as Collateral With the Bank or With Another Lender?

If you can use the company's assets as collateral, you can keep your own cash investment in the purchase at a minimum. For example, if the business has a backlog of orders for the product it produces, you can take those orders to the bank to secure the financing necessary to purchase the operation, since the orders show that you will be able to repay the loan.

HOW TO SPOT IT/TEST IT/PACKAGE IT WHEN THE INVESTMENT IS A FRANCHISE

If you're considering a franchise, you need to determine whether this specific enterprise is a more attractive option than opening a similar independent operation that's not under someone else's banner.

70

1. What Is the Success Record of the Overall Franchise?

Background and track record are all-important when considering the purchase of a franchise. Ask the franchisor for a complete rundown on its business history and success record. If the company and/or franchise are publicly held, that information will be available in the prospectus or annual report. Realize that the strongest assets of a franchise are the reputation of the company, its expertise, know-how, and goodwill. An investor in a McDonald's franchise, for example, isn't buying ground beef and buns. The asset is the McDonald's name, the confidence that name evokes in the consumer, the goodwill among investors, and the massive advertising and public relations benefits that accrue with the McDonald's name.

2. What Does the Franchise Package Include?

Not all franchise deals are the same. Some, such as McDonald's, include a complete business package that can't be modified or adjusted—your investment gives you a tested moneymaking plan, but you're required to follow that plan to the letter. Other franchise arrangements offer you a name, a business, a location, and not much more, while still others give you varying degrees of independence. It is essential that you determine the precise arrangements of the franchise you are considering—and that you're certain you're comfortable with those arrangements.

3. Will the Franchisor Train You and Your Employees?

The dividing line between success and failure in a franchise operation is often the level of training that is provided to its employees and management. An example of a topflight training program is that of PIP (Postal Instant Press), a nationwide franchise operation offering quick duplicating and printing services for documents. The company puts all franchisees through an extensive training program at the home office in Los Angeles. Graduates of that program know the business inside and out and are well equipped to make a success of the franchise. They also know they are backed by an operation they can call upon whenever they run into a problem—another important thing to consider.

4. Does the Franchisor Provide Financial Assistance or Participate in Obtaining Financing for the Operations?

The franchising company has a value in the marketplace and is sometimes willing to provide assistance in securing financing for the franchisee. Some companies even offer their own financing. Check to see if these services are available.

5. What Do Other Franchisees Say About the Operation?

Ask for the names, addresses, and phone numbers of at least five other franchisees, and then contact them to find out how satisfied they've been with their operation. Ask about revenues, problems, and other inside tidbits of information.

6. Is This Franchise a New Offering or a Resale of an Existing Location?

Be wary of resales of existing franchises. Really profitable operations are rarely resold, and even if the owner needs to dispose of the property, the franchisor usually will take over a money-maker. Find out why the business is for sale—it might present problems you don't want to tackle.

7. Does the Franchise Suit Your Particular Investment Personality?

If your career has been spent as an accountant or in some other analytical line of work, then a franchise that requires you to operate in an outgoing, sales-oriented mode might be a mismatch. Matching an investment vehicle with your personality is essential.

CHAPTER 4

PTP: Put Yourself in a Position to Profit

Hotel executive Sandra Peters came to me not long ago to ask for help in designing a plan that would enable her to reach her financial goals. Everything about her spelled success—everything except her bank account.

While she made what she once would have considered to be a good salary, she was hardly getting by. She couldn't afford to buy a house or condominium, nor could she create any other tax write-offs.

As she explained her situation to me, I could see why. She was profit-blocked. Her moneymaking activities had unwittingly become structured for financial failure, and no matter how smart she was, how hard she worked, or how many hours she put in, her financial bottom line would stay the same. My goal was to take her through the three steps necessary to put herself in a position to profit:

rethinking, repackaging, and *restructuring* her skills and assets.

I began by getting more information. Sandra was then earning $35,000 as head of marketing and sales for a medium-sized hotel in a plush Los Angeles suburb. As she told me about her job, I could see that there was no place for her to go in the company's management. The only spot higher than hers was that of president/general manager—a position that was held by the company's owner.

I also learned that, while she had received numerous offers from other hotels to take over their marketing duties, she had stayed with her company because the hotel where she worked was considered a gem and her job was, as she put it, "one that anyone would give their eyeteeth for."

Beautiful surroundings are usually costly, I said, and asked her to tell me about those other offers.

One was with a hotel that was still under construction in a semiindustrial section of Orange County, a far cry from the Bel Air work environment she enjoyed so much. While the job offered only an additional $5,000 a year in salary, I encouraged her to consider it because of the opportunity it provided to work for an entrepreneur who had a reputation for challenging his employees with virtually limitless responsibilities—and opportunities.

Realizing that she had to give up her posh surroundings to position herself for profit, Sandra took the new position, going from the comfort of a "gem" hotel to wearing a hard hat and working out of a trailer on the construction site for six months. But the move paid off. When the new hotel became a tremendous success, the owner of the company gave her a $5,000 bonus plus the opportunity to head marketing activities for all his other ventures. She negotiated a profit-sharing arrangement and, in the span of one year, took her income from $35,000 to $85,000.

And there's more.

Sandra had mentioned to me that she usually received from three to five requests each month to do consulting work. I suggested that she set up a private consulting service in her extra time, handling clients who didn't compete with her employer's line of business. She is now making an additional $15,000 a year in consulting fees, and the establishment of her own business has also given her excellent tax write-offs.

In all areas of her professional life, Sandra is now perfectly positioned to profit:

- The harder and smarter she works, the more profit she derives from her efforts.
- There is no limit on her income potential.
- Her financial earnings are structured for minimum taxes.
- She has affiliated with top financial performers—and she profits as they profit.
- She has automated her investments.
- She has the assets and the attitude necessary

to seize potential moneymaking situations that appear within her Economic Orbit of Opportunity.

Sandra didn't get into this position through an act of legerdemain or other magic. She began to rethink her goals, to repackage her skills, and to restructure her moneymaking activities through a series of steps you'll learn in this chapter.

RETHINKING YOUR GOALS

Your first step in putting yourself in a position to profit is to rethink exactly what you want to achieve in terms of short- and long-range money goals, as well as what abilities you have to take you where you want to go.

If you're like most people, you do quite well at setting and reaching goals on the job. But you've undoubtedly never thought of using that same technique in terms of your own moneymaking activities because, with the exception of bills and taxes, there really aren't any hard and fast deadlines in the financial area of your life. There aren't any timetables you have to follow in terms of earning a better salary, creating financial security, or getting rich, so it's relatively easy to just drift and dream. But, as Spencer Johnson, author of *The One-Minute Manager*, put it, goals are nothing more than dreams with a deadline. To put yourself in a position to profit, you need to start setting goals for financial success and then creating the structures that will enable you to meet them.

One of the main reasons why corporations like IBM, Delta Airlines, and Xerox Corporation are so successful is that they take the process of goal-setting very seriously. Long- and short-range goals are developed, considered, modified, and updated. And, most important, they're consistently attained. With a few modifications, that same technique can help you get what you want in the money world.

While I readily admit that one of the biggest problems in goal-setting is the nearly unlimited range of options to choose from (an intimidating thought, at best), I guarantee that the very process of choosing and prioritizing goals will force you to channel your energy into avenues with the greatest potential for positive return—which is really what profit is all about.

As I tell my clients and lecture audiences, you need to establish your goals in terms of three time frames: (1) short range (one year), (2) intermediate range (three years), and (3) long range (five years or more). Within each time frame, pinpoint in specific terms what you'd like to achieve. Would you like to be driving a Mercedes in one year? Do you want the down payment for a new home in three years? Do you want to be able to quit your job and go into business for yourself? When? Or would you be content to accumulate enough extra cash to go on a big vacation now and then? Only you can decide what

you really want—and when you want it. And now's
the time to make that decision.

YOUR PERSONAL GOALS INVENTORY

Filling out your Personal Goals Inventory forces
you to begin focusing on what you want, when you
want it, and the vehicles you can use for achieving
those goals. It takes into consideration the amount
of time you're prepared to devote to making money
and how long you're willing to wait to achieve your
goals, as well as the emotional aspects of moneymaking.

1. What Are My Emotional Needs in Terms of Money?

Before you begin to set dollar figures for what you'd
like to achieve financially, you need to understand
your economic personality and how you respond to
money on an emotional level. How important to
you is safety in terms of investments? Have there
been financial traumas in your life that have made
you cautious about money? Would you like to feel
more financially secure than you do today? Or are
you a gambler who is willing to take a course of
action that is a bit more risky? Does talking about
money make you nervous, or are you relatively
matter-of-fact? Do you see repeated patterns in

your financial life that cause you emotional distress?

On the first page of your Goals Inventory, write a paragraph or two explaining how you feel about money and financial security.

2. What Do I Really Want to Achieve Financially?

Now's the time to describe your dreams and write down your financial "want list." Are you at the starting gate in terms of buying your first house? Do you wish you had more money in the bank? Do you want to get involved in different types of investments than those you have traditionally pursued? Putting a few paragraphs under this question on your Goals Inventory will force you to take a look at where you really want to go.

3. What Is My Time Framework?

What do you want to accomplish in one year, three years, five years, and even twenty years? And how much time are you willing to devote to reaching those financial goals? Be honest with yourself—don't write down that you're willing to throw yourself wholeheartedly into moneymaking when you know that you'd really rather spend your weekends on the tennis court.

One of my clients is a writer who decided while taking her Goals Inventory that she wanted to be making an additional $10,000 a year and was willing to devote two weekends a month to reaching that goal. Taking that time structure into consideration, she then decided she could reasonably expect to produce two magazine articles a month at an anticipated earnings of $500 per article. Setting a dollar amount and a time frame for reaching it gave her the structure she needed to accomplish her goal.

4. What Was My Most Successful Investment (of Time, Money, or Expertise) During the Past Ten Years?

Whether your most successful investment was your education, your home, a tax-free bond, or a venture capital deal, take a moment to identify it and figure out why it worked out so well. Try to determine whether your success was due to luck or to particular insights, skills, or expertise you've developed in this specific area.

5. What Was My Least Successful Investment During the Past Ten Years?

Under this heading list those investments that haven't paid off and try to determine what it was that made them flop. For example, did you lose a bundle in the stock market because you went into speculative new issues without recognizing the high-risk factor?

The purpose of this exercise is to find the financial strategies that will offer you the greatest moneymaking potential with the highest degree of comfort. Choosing a financial strategy is a lot like buying a pair of shoes—you have to find one that feels comfortable or else you'll only be miserable, no matter how attractive it looks to everyone else.

PUTTING YOUR GOALS INVENTORY TO WORK

The following six-step process will help you take your goals from dreams to reality:

1. Write Down a Goal That You Want to Achieve

Do you want more money in the bank, a bigger house, a better job, more tax write-offs?

2. Quantify That Goal

How much money do you want in the bank? What kind of a house? What kind of investments?

3. Qualify That Goal

What deadline can you set that's realistic and yet a challenge? Divide the goal and the time frame into reasonable chunks.

4. Identify the Vehicle for Reaching the Goal

Do you have a hobby that you think could turn into a money-maker? Can you use your payroll-deduction plan to amass a healthy bank account? Do you have an invention you can test and market? This is the time to decide upon the method you'll use to reach your financial goal.

5. Go Through the Conversion Process

Do the groundwork for setting your plan in motion. Find out more about the investments you want to pursue or determine the market for the product you plan to produce. Identify experts who can help you achieve your plan and get them involved in the process.

6. Take Instant Action Toward That Goal

You'll learn more about how to apply my concept of instant action in Chapter 9, HALT: High Action/Low Talk.

GETTING MORE COMFORTABLE
WITH GOAL-SETTING

There are a number of little tricks you can use to become more comfortable with setting and reaching goals. For example, try establishing some small goals you are confident you can achieve within a short period of time. The success you'll feel from those accomplishments will give you the confidence to try others that are more ambitious.

Or you could try what I call the Salami Approach—cut the project up into manageable slices and take it one slice at a time. That's how a runner approaches a race, and it's how I go about writing a book. I develop a theme and a rough outline and then I take it one chapter at a time. By breaking a project down into smaller chunks, it's less intimidating and you gain momentum as you move along.

The blank check is another "trick" you can use to get more comfortable with goal-setting. Take a blank check out of your checkbook and write yourself a check in the amount you'd like to earn each year. Take another check and fill it out for the amount you'd like to have in a savings account. Make out another for the amount you'd like to have as your net worth. Put these checks in a file that you

label "Goals," and check on your progress from
time to time.

REPACKAGING YOUR SKILLS

Once you've rethought your money goals and the
assets (skills, expertise, contacts, and finances) you
have at your command to achieve them, you're
ready to repackage those assets at their highest,
best, and broadest level, to turn seemingly lateral
career moves into money-makers, and to go from
merely earning a paycheck to having a piece of the
action.

HIGHEST, BEST, AND BROADEST USE

In real estate it's standard procedure to make decisions based upon the highest and best use of a
parcel of land. For example, the highest and best
use of a piece of property on Rodeo Drive and
Wilshire Boulevard in Beverly Hills or at Fifth Avenue and 59th Street in New York City certainly
wouldn't be a single-family home. It would take a
fifty-story office building to make maximum use of
the land.

The same concept can be applied to your assets

and skills. Are they being used to their highest, best, and broadest use? Or, like a small house located on a prime piece of commercial real estate, are you making minimal use of something with maximum value?

Barbara Ryan-Baylor had worked for fifteen years as a volunteer fund-raiser for a major university until a divorce forced her to repackage her expertise and contacts into a profit-making operation. Thinking of her skills in terms of highest, best, and broadest use, she began to see the value of the access she enjoyed to top charitable contributors all across the country, as well as to community members who regularly participate in and plan fund-raising events. She started her own business doing fund-raising consultations for a variety of nonprofit institutions, including colleges and universities across the country. She's still using the same skills she's practiced for the past fifteen years, only now they're being used to benefit a number of educational institutions instead of just one, and providing her with a comfortable living as well.

LATERAL MOVES AND QUANTUM LEAPS

The shortest distance between two points, we're told, is a straight line. In the corporate world, it would then make sense that a straight line would be up. But today, with the middle-management ranks filled with baby boomers in their thirties and early forties, routine movement up the corporate ladder is going to be slow, if not statistically impossible. The "straight line"—or shortest distance— might just be a lateral move, as in football where the quarterback passes across, not down, the field to an open spot, where the receiver can then make a run for the goal line.

In the corporate arena, that lateral move is also to a less crowded ladder. I have a theory that the best way to the top is to step off the ladder itself, pull it away from its resting place, put it under your arm, and carry it to the spot of your choice— that way you're in charge of the ladder and where you do your climbing.

My suggestion to hotel executive Sandra Peters was she take her ladder to a new arena—in the less glamorous section of Orange County. She's a perfect example of a person who made what appears to be a lateral move—only to end up with a quantum leap.

PAYCHECK TO PAYCHECK PLUS

Moving from paycheck to paycheck plus means seeing your career potential as open-ended, with the potential for a piece of the action—your own action.

A good example is Trish Woodrich, a graphics expert who had been with one of the major television studios for ten years when she decided to open her own graphics consulting firm in her free time. The consulting work became so lucrative that she scaled down her hours with the production company to a part-time basis. That move has turned out to be a smart one, since it allows the production company access to her talent at a fraction of her former salary while still giving her the freedom to pursue additional work—and a far greater income—through her own company.

I first met Lynne Ross when she was working in the publicity department of a major New York publishing house. As we got to know each other, she told me about her frustrations with East Coast living and the dead-end financial situation she was experiencing with her job. I knew her reputation as one of the top publicists in the country, and suggested that she reposition her profit potential by becoming a consultant to her current employer. She could then accept a number of clients and multiply her income. Since a significant portion of the book publicizing business is now taking place on the West Coast, I also suggested that she base her consulting service in California and pick up additional clients there. Although she thought her employers would never go for the idea, they readily agreed to her terms (since they'd be paying her less as a consultant than as a regular employee and knew they wouldn't be losing access to her skills).

She took my advice and now has public relations offices in Los Angeles and San Francisco, in addition to one in New York. After seven years, her former employer is still one of her best clients.

More and more people who used to be satisfied with a weekly paycheck are finding that they want to pursue entrepreneurial activities on their own. Of course there will be problems along the way as they juggle their priorities in order to achieve a balance that they and their employers can live with, but such arrangements can be beneficial to all concerned when a healthy balance has been reached.

Chuck Alpers was a restaurant-management specialist for a large hotel chain, overseeing and directing fine dining facilities in a number of cities before being transferred to the East Coast, a few years ago. When another relocation seemed imminent, he decided to go for "paycheck plus" instead of a secure paycheck with a major corporation, and went to work for what has become a stunningly successful new restaurant in the area. His decision to put himself in a position to profit has meant a considerable jump in pay and perks, a piece of the action—and the enormous satisfaction of being in control of his own destiny.

RESTRUCTURING YOURSELF FOR PROFIT

This is the action-oriented step that will allow you to put your rethinking and repackaging into effect. Restructuring involves five procedures:

> Automate
> Delegate
> Affiliate
> Create
> Terminate

which can be used singly or in tandem to help you complete your profit repositioning.

Automate

To achieve your goals, particularly if they're long-term, you need to either automate the process of achieving them or delegate the achievement to someone with more time or expertise.

The automation process can be as simple as setting up a payroll deduction plan with your employer or your bank. Any kind of enforced payment plan will help you automate achievement of your goals, including insurance policy premiums, a mortgage on a home, or other programs with monthly deadlines that force you to meet a specific commitment. A noted New York stockbroker and financial planner even went so far as to suggest borrowing to begin investing, explaining that the payback process gives a quick impetus to financial action and creates a forced repayment with money that is being "prudently" invested in higher yielding investments. Again, the emphasis is on automating; in this instance the automation is in the repayment of the loan.

You can automate savings and you can automate a mortgage. You can't, however, automate any major entrepreneurial moneymaking venture. That is a quite different dimension, but there is no reason why you cannot be involved in both kinds of activities at the same time.

Delegate

Delegating the process of achieving your goals often involves teamwork, with each member of the team contributing a different strength. Stan Lindley was relatively unsophisticated in respect to financial matters, so he decided to team up with a friend who's a financial wizard, matching his friend's expertise with his own cash investment. The two have now invested in close to ten different properties around Southern California, leveraging Stan's cash and his friend's skill into a sizable real estate portfolio.

Of course, delegation should never be a "blind-trust" situation. Few people can afford to completely turn over all details and responsibilities of their financial planning to someone else. By "delegate," I mean working in conjunction with a professional or a qualified friend to get your goals achieved.

Affiliate

Another method of achieving your goals is to affiliate with others who have a proven record of financial success. They don't have to be big-money people but simply those who have made consistently wise moves over a period of time. David Fellows, a man I worked with a number of years ago, became an expert in the area of small real-estate acquisitions, none of which exceeded the $150,000 mark. He began to put together shared small-equity situations and worked with investors who had $2,000 to $2,500 to deal with, combining their assets to accomplish what none of them could do alone.

I keep my eyes open for people like David because there are great opportunities for success by affiliating with those who are well informed, successful, and actively involved in looking into new deals. Partnerships in the financial area offer an excellent way to begin the moneymaking process. I personally know of many people who began by team investing and made significant gains in knowledge and expertise, whether or not they made a financial killing. (See Chapter 5 for more details on team investing.)

Create

Financial success, as you know, does not happen by mistake or by luck. It does happen by design. The design, however, has to be created.

The creation process involves developing a structure—whether it's a real estate investment, an insurance policy, or a savings program—to achieve your financial goals.

My friend Deborah Carletti had a goal of creating a net worth of $250,000. We discussed the various financial investment structures that would allow her to achieve that goal with little or no risk and virtually no investment of time. After we evaluated her various personal preferences, she decided that her expertise in interior design and architecture pointed to real estate as the vehicle. Because of her time constraints as a sales manager with a small computer-software company, she chose to get involved in a team investment in real estate, which was less time consuming than doing it alone. Her sister and a friend who's a real estate appraiser decided to join her in a share equity (team investment) in a four-plex in San Diego, California.

The $250,000 price tag was steep and required a $50,000 down payment. As it turned out, they put down only 5 percent, and the seller retained a $45,000 second mortgage—interest only for the first five years. (The seller didn't want to pay taxes on the lump sum and was happy to get 14 percent interest on his $45,000.)

Deborah's creation of a moneymaking structure became the catalyst for a series of investment moves. (I've seen this happen repeatedly—once the initial investment decision is made and implemented, the barrier is broken and a new sense of confidence arises.) Within eight months of the first investment, Deborah became involved in four other income-property deals, each requiring only infinitesimal down payments and offering long-standing tenants.

Deanna Fry decided to take a different route. As an ace executive secretary for twenty-three years, Deanna was the typist I hired when I was drafting my second book a few years back. Her goal was to parlay her twenty-three years' experience in the secretarial field into a business of her own, but the thought of a typing service didn't appeal to her. She wanted an entity that would increase in value, and one that would also function without her constant supervision. As we went through the options, the concept of a franchise became more and more attractive to her. We discussed the various types, from McDonald's to service stations, and I told her about Postal Instant Press (PIP), a company I'd checked out while researching a story for "The Today Show."

Deanna was intrigued and called their corporate headquarters in Beverly Hills to talk with their franchise manager. They met, discussed location openings, franchise requirements, financing assistance, and training programs. It became clear that Deanna liked the idea of being involved with a proven winner. She began her PIP franchise operation with $55,000 and sold it seven years later for $250,000. Hers has become a two-in-one situation—locking in a good income that's twice what she was making while creating a comfortable resale value for her retirement. It seems doubtful that she will be retiring for some time, though. She has just invested in her third franchise in partnership with her son and daughter.

Terminate

It may surprise you, but one essential to achieving your financial goals is clearing away the obstacles that might be standing in your way. One such obstacle could be a business relationship in which there is a mismatch of goals.

Jerry Kitchell had been in the executive placement field for ten years and was considered to be one of the top people in this highly profitable business. His partner was totally committed to staying in the personnel area, while new horizons were opening up to Jerry, who was becoming fascinated with management-consulting opportunities. His reputation brought him to the attention of top-level executives who called on him for advice on a wide range of corporate and personnel issues, including strategic planning and acquisitions.

His dilemma was lack of time to handle his widening duties, as well as his partner's insistence that he continue to devote time to the personnel and executive-recruitment activities.

As we went over his financial goals, which included heading a $5-million consulting firm, it became clear that this goal could not be achieved in his current partnership arrangement. Essential to achieving his financial goal was restructuring his partnership—terminating the relationship but continuing to share office space while pursuing new paths. The painful but necessary termination of the partnership has doubled each of their annual incomes, since they're both doing what they really want to do—and doing it well.

CHAPTER 5

NCR: No Cash Required

While it's true that you need cash to start most business ventures, the cash you use doesn't necessarily have to be your own. You don't have to *have* money to go into business, you just have to have *access* to money. And, fortunately, there are now more traditional and nontraditional sources for securing start-up cash than ever before.

In this chapter, however, I'm not as interested in providing you with a long list of funding sources as I am in teaching you how to develop creative, imaginative strategies for approaching those sources—strategies that will make the difference between success and failure in getting the money you need. By the time you finish reading this chapter, I hope you'll realize that when you have a good idea for a product or service, there's always a way to get the financing to back it.

Perhaps the most innovative approach to raising

business capital was that of Andy Lipkis, founder of the Tree People, who had a great idea but no money to get it launched. He was concerned about the deterioration of the environment and began a nonprofit project to plant smog-resistant trees in California forests to slow the browning of the landscape from pollution. He also had a plan to slow soil erosion by using volunteers to plant seedlings on hillsides that had been ravaged by California's notorious fall brush fires—an idea that would save the state the millions of dollars it ordinarily spent each year having forestry employees carry out that function.

Andy's idea seemed like a natural to receive grant money or funding from the state or federal government, but no matter how hard he tried, he couldn't get a penny.

Frustrated, Andy started pleading his case with the news media, letting reporters know how his project would benefit the environment. He ended up telling his story on television news and talk shows—and his tactic worked. He soon received the money he needed from private funding sources plus the Environmental Educational Fund and the California Division of Forestry.

You can be similarly creative in acquiring the funding you need to bring your idea to the marketplace. Listed here are a dozen of my favorite ways to raise capital.

ELEVEN WAYS TO GET MONEY FOR YOUR VENTURE

1. Cash in Advance

Rory Feurst, whose tennis shoe resoling operation made entrepreneurial history, spent five months at his parents' kitchen table trying different techniques and materials to come up with a way to apply new soles to used tennis shoes. After he had perfected his process, he began to follow the obvious routes to secure funding for a resoling company, including filling out an application for a business loan. When his bank told him his idea was too risky for them to take a chance on, he asked his family and friends if they would lend him the money to get started, but they simply didn't have any extra capital to invest.

So Rory decided to go directly to his potential customers. He went to the local tennis courts each weekend and spotted people who had tennis shoes with worn-out soles. He walked up to them, told them about his new retreading process, and offered to rejuvenate their shoes for $6.50—in advance. He went to every tennis court in town and ended up with enough orders and money to begin his resoling operation.

Then he expanded upon his Cash in Advance funding method by placing an advertisement in *Sports Illustrated*, telling people that if they'd send him their worn-out tennis shoes and a check for $6.50, he'd quickly return the shoes as good as new. For nearly a month, Rory and his two (unpaid) assistants waited anxiously for responses to the ad. They didn't get a single reply until one Friday afternoon they'll probably never forget. The postman rang Rory's doorbell and told him that there was a truck at the curb filled with 3,200 pairs of smelly tennis shoes. Each one of those pairs was accompanied by a $6.50 check, which meant that Rory had more than $20,000 in working capital to launch his venture.

I showed a woman I met at a seminar in Dayton, Ohio, how to use a similar approach to fund her business venture. She was a nutritionist who had developed a highly structured food plan that had helped many of her friends and associates lose weight and maintain that loss. She decided to open her own business, preparing meals based upon her food plan and hiring students to deliver them to her clients, who would pay her $350 a month for the service. I worked with her to develop a strategy so she could get the $350 monthly fee from her subscribers at the *beginning* of each month, rather than the end, as she had planned. She advertised her service at the local exercise classes, the YWCA, and various women's groups around town. Within a few weeks, she had 100 clients—and $35,000 in start-up capital.

Cash in Advance is a commonly used method of raising venture capital, and it's also one of my favorites.

2. The De Lorean Method

In analyses of car-maker John De Lorean's business failure, most observers overlook the brilliant and innovative first step he took to secure capital for his company.

In his initial search for raising approximately $500 million in capital, he decided that he would require each potential distributor to become an investor in his company. He explained that the terms for becoming a De Lorean distributor included a $35,000 investment upon signing of the distribution agreement. This was a highly unusual approach, but one that worked. That money went into building factories, manufacturing the De Lorean car, and taking care of basic corporate costs.

You can use this same concept to develop funding for your product or service if you're using a distribution system made up of individuals who could become distributors/investors.

3. Cash for Order

I recently met with two manufacturers who were trying to raise $2.5 million to produce an excellent but fairly expensive supermarket refrigeration system they had designed. As we discussed the various methods of raising capital and the time frame they had to work with, I suggested that they use the Cash for Order approach. Since they had already received several orders for their product from major supermarket chains, I advised them to go to those stores to negotiate additional orders for delivery during the next twelve to eighteen months. The orders could then be taken to the bank and used as collateral for a substantial loan because they would indicate that the company had a strong future and every likelihood of being able to pay off the loan. Because the supermarket executives liked the refrigeration system, and knew that placing orders for future delivery would guarantee next year's delivery at this year's prices, they agreed to the deal. The manufacturers presented their signed contracts to the bank and received the $2.5 million they needed.

This method of raising capital, which is also called "the sponsor method" or "the proof of repayment approach," can be used with virtually any bank or lending institution in the country, as well as with independent investors, family, and friends. All you need is a signed contract indicating a promise of future payment from a well-established company with a respectable Dun and Bradstreet rating.

4. The Cheering Section—or Vested Interests

One of the most commonly overlooked sources of funding for new products, services, companies, and real estate ventures is family and friends and those with vested interests in the venture. Of course there's always the concern about what would happen to a personal relationship if you found yourself unable to repay the loan. But, even with this consideration in mind, you might want to offer those close to you the opportunity to make some money on your venture.

I was recently in Jacksonville, Florida, giving a speech, and a local businesswoman in the audience raised her hand and asked for advice on handling the rejection she met in trying to secure financial backing for her company. When I asked her how many times she had been turned down, she dropped her eyes, lowered her head, and said, "I've already had two people say they weren't interested. I really hate the rejection process."

I explained that two turndowns are sometimes only the beginning when you're searching for funding, adding that you should be prepared to make dozens of presentations before you get the right match between the investor's interest and your project.

Then I asked whether her family or friends had indicated an interest in backing her operation. She looked a bit surprised, then said that four or five friends had already done so.

"And I bet you haven't approached any of them," I said.

"You're absolutely right," she admitted.

I suggested that she begin her new search for backers by telephoning those who had already indicated an interest in investing in her company. I told her it was my bet that by the time she had made her third telephone call, she'd have the money she needed.

During a seminar in Dallas, Texas, several months ago, I met a woman who needed expansion capital for her company, called The Cookie Lady, which produces and sells original-recipe cookies in a local shopping mall.

As we talked, she told me about the many people who came into her shop and asked for recipes after they tasted the cookies she baked. Quite a few, she said, were tourists from all over the country who told her that there was nothing like her operation where they lived. Many had even asked if they could buy a franchise for their city, but she had always said that there were no franchises available because hers was a one-woman operation.

I asked how many franchise inquiries she had received.

"Oh, maybe two hundred," she said. "I've kept all their names in this file."

"Two hundred! They're your unofficial Cheering Section. There's your financing right there," I said, suggesting that she start a letter-writing campaign to contact all the people who had asked about franchises, requesting more information about their interest and their qualifications. I told her that she could then meet with franchising experts to map out how she could replicate her cookie shops all over the country. Asking her more questions, I found out that a local supermarket had expressed interest in offering her packaged cookie dough to their customers. I advised her to take the supermarket up on its offer and also to pursue the franchise arrangements, both of which would add significant sums to the expansion money she was pulling together. I received a letter from her a few weeks ago, telling me she had already contacted at least fifty potential franchisees.

5. The Team Investing Method—All for One and One for All

So often I hear people in my audiences say, "I'd love to buy a piece of real estate or a house of my own—but I don't have the money." I tell them that teamwork can make their dreams come true.

A good example of the successful application of Team Investing is the story of Jan Michaels, a stewardess whose job had already allowed her to work and play her way around the world for eighteen years when we met during one of my seminars in the Los Angeles area. She told me that until a few months earlier she had felt that her money was to be spent—and that's what she had done. Clothes, shoes, jewelry, and vacations had eaten up nearly every penny she had made during her career. She said she'd begun to question her priorities during a recent flight from Chicago, when another stewardess was enthusiastically talking about her new condominium—and her plans to buy and rent out many more.

Jan said that she'd gotten furious with herself for all those years of making good money with little to show for it. She told me that she'd already turned her anger into action by taking a quick tour of local condominiums with a real estate broker. She saw a unit she liked, but was met with a cool response when she told the broker she didn't have the down payment.

"Let me know when you get the cash," she was told.

Jan asked me for any advice I might have on how to start investing her money, even though she had little to work with.

I suggested that she contact a number of friends and associates to see if they'd be interested in a team investment, with each putting in a portion of the sum needed for the down payment on the condo in return for a share of the investment. She soon had three candidates who were pleased to put in $5,000 in return for a piece of the action. While none of them were rich, they all had good-paying jobs and passable credit, so they had no trouble securing a loan. Jan's job seniority alone was music to the bank's ears. Jan and her three partners bought the condominium and rented it out to a long-term tenant.

"We had the condo rented from the day the escrow was closed," she told me a few weeks ago, adding that the four investors have formed a partnership with monthly meetings to discuss various real estate opportunities, tax benefit strategies, and potential expansion to other properties.

Another example of team investing is the story of David Baldwin, a lab technician in the office of several Chicago doctors. David noticed that the doctors were constantly talking about real estate deals and tax shelters, but had little time to act upon their interest. Since he had plenty of spare time and not much money, he came up with a proposal for a unique arrangement—he suggested that he receive a 7 percent cut for the time he would spend in structuring real-estate investment deals for the doctors.

Since they knew that he had taken quite a few classes in real estate management and had worked closely with them in making major purchases of expensive equipment for the office, they were aware that he had an extremely analytical mind and a solid business sense, so they agreed to his suggestion. He became their investment sleuth in exchange for participation in each of the deals.

David began spending his evenings and weekends evaluating various properties until he found several that were good deals. The doctors had their attorney check the terms of the investments, and she agreed that they were good opportunities. The last time I talked with him, David told me that this arrangement had turned into a very profitable use of his time and the doctors' money.

6. The Tom Sawyer Approach

One of the biggest operating costs for any business is the payroll. Many new companies simply don't have much in their budget to pay salaries during the initial months of operation. If that description fits your business, you might consider following the example of Mark Twain's Tom Sawyer, who, you may remember, got all his friends involved in the fence-painting chores he was supposed to perform.

In a business situation, my Tom Sawyer Approach involves an exchange of stock in the company in payment for services performed. For example, if you've come up with an idea for a new computer program and need to have someone design the software, you could offer a piece of the action in the form of stock or stock and cash instead of a traditional cash payment.

7. The Barter Approach

Another variation on the Tom Sawyer Approach involves exchanging either goods or services for what you need. For example, Christine Batten is a Minneapolis graphic artist who provided free signs for a year to an art supply store in exchange for the equipment she needed to start her own design firm. Stephanie Keyser, who recently opened a new restaurant in Philadelphia, provides four free dinners each month to the woman who does her accounting chores.

Take a good look at your skills and the products and services you have at your disposal. I'm sure you'll see similar opportunities.

8. The Piggyback Approach

If your idea, venture, or company doesn't have the necessary strength to serve as the basis for getting a business loan or any other fund-generating arrangement, you can use the Piggyback Approach and bring in a cosigner who will lend weight to your credibility.

Ellen Lucero is a Dallas attorney who was involved in time-consuming research for a number of asbestos-related pollution cases she was handling. She needed $200,000 in working capital to cover her office rent and pay her secretarial staff until she received what she knew would be sizable fees based upon a percentage of the damages her clients would collect. She wrote up a business plan and took it to her bank to ask for a loan. She was told that the bank would look more favorably upon her application if she had a cosigner, so she approached a friend and offered to pay her $1,000 for her signature as backup on the deal. Ellen got the loan with that extra signature on her application.

9. Pilot-Project Approach

A pilot project is clearly worth a thousand words and can be the deciding factor in getting your funding.

By pilot project I mean an action plan that demonstrates your ability to get something done. It could involve putting together a sample chapter for a book, coming up with a miniature design of a solar panel house that you have constructed, or showing a sample of previous computer programs that you may have put together. In effect, a pilot project shows not only that you can accomplish what you say you can, but also that you're willing to translate your abilities into action. Demonstrating the ability to get things done will impress an investor more than all the flip charts, graphs, and beautifully worded statements you could offer.

10. A Piece of the Action—Venture Capital

The question I'm most often asked about venture capital is, "Is venture capital really available for people like me or is it only there for people who have the next Apple Computer or a no-calorie cookie?"

Let's get a couple of things straight about venture capital:

1. Venture capitalists are interested only in deals that typically return a ratio of 5 to 1. That means for every dollar they put in, they're expecting a $5 return on their money, typically within an eighteen-month period.

Venture capitalists are also looking for the placement of large dollars—$500,000 and up. Many venture capitalists are interested only in placements in excess of $1 million to $5 million.

2. The lion's share of venture capital money is going for high technology because that's where the potential for maximum return is, particularly in electronics or medical areas where one breakthrough can be turned into a profit millions and millions of times over, such as with the invention of Valium, or the birth control pill by Syntex Corpo-

ration. But some venture capital is generally available for low-tech as well as high-tech ventures.

3. Virtually all venture capitalists want, not just a piece of the action, but a *significant* piece of the action. This means that they're not interested in just lending you money. They want part of the ownership—or equity—of a company in exchange for providing the backing, because they're expecting not only the return of their original capital but also the famous 5 to 1 capital return.

4. High-tech or low, there are venture capitalists for virtually every type of deal. However, matching up your venture with the right venture capitalists is perhaps the most critical element in the deal other than having a basically fundable investment.

Let me give you a clear example. If you look at any standard directory of venture capital sources, you'll find that each is looking for different types of ventures to participate in. This means that some are looking for real estate investments, some are looking for film deals, some are looking for high-tech manufacturing, and others are looking only for service industries to invest in. So, when you're searching for potential venture capitalists who would be interested in your particular kind of deal, remember that a good business proposal matched with the right venture capitalist can net a deal made in heaven.

The best source I know of that fully describes the venture capital market is the *Corporate Finance Source Book*. It's very expensive, selling for approximately $395 a copy, so I suggest that you go to your local library to look up the particular venture capital category you're interested in, since most libraries with good business sections have a copy of this volume. You might also be able to use a copy at your local bank.

11. Writing for Dollars—From Hot Air to Cold Facts

A business plan is the basic difference between hot air and cold facts. It is a crucial ingredient in any fund-raising endeavor.

I consulted recently with a group of Los Angeles film producers who were looking for venture capital to finance their films. They spent three-and-a-half hours telling me all about their production company and what they were planning to accomplish.

I explained to them that while their project was fascinating and their track record was excellent, there were hundreds of other film deals and equivalent investments being offered to investors throughout the country at that particular moment. I told them they needed to make their deal stand out from all the others—and one way to do that was to put their specific investment plan on paper in the form of a *business plan* they could present to potential investors. Until they were willing to do that, they'd find few investors who would devote three-and-a-half hours to listening to the facts, figures, and promises of their scheme.

114

The same advice applies to you if you have a deal to offer to investors, particularly if it requires huge financing or involves an "intangible" product. In those circumstances, there's only one way to go, and that's to write up a business plan. During the past ten years, I've assisted dozens of companies to get funded, for a total of more than $100 million. Each of those deals was successful because of a carefully developed business plan. It takes skill to write a business plan that accurately and succinctly presents the relevant information about your particular venture, but it's a skill that you can quickly learn. In the Appendix, I have provided an outline you can follow to write a business plan for your venture.

CHAPTER 6

PAPA: Profitable Attitude/ Profitable Action

One of my favorite stories about making money concerns three people who were each given a chance to win a million dollars from a large conglomerate. All they had to do was to take a look at an unusual parcel of land and within three days tell the conglomerate how much money they would need to implement a profitable use of the land. The person with the best profit-to-cost ratio would get his or her idea developed and receive the million-dollar reward.

The land resembled a small, tropical version of the Grand Canyon. It was mountainous, rimmed by steep cliffs. A white river rapid ran through the center of the 500-acre parcel, with a rope bridge spanning its width. The temperature hovered around eighty degrees all year long.

The first person presented his proposal. "I think the location and weather would make the area ideal for a resort hotel," he said. "I'll need two million dollars for a feasibility study of the area. I can make my final recommendations within ninety days."

The second person then made his presentation. His proposal was half as expensive, but just as ambitious. "I'll need one million for a geological study of possible mineral deposits of gold, iron ore, and platinum," he said.

The third person took everyone by surprise when she said, "Gentlemen, all I'll need is one hundred dollars—or an American Express card—for my million-dollar venture."

The conglomerate's tycoons were intrigued. "What can you possibly do with a hundred dollars?" they asked.

"Buy two sawhorses, a piece of rope, and a twelve-foot two-by-four."

"How would that make us money?"

"You know that bridge up there?" she asked. "I sat there for the past three days and counted more than five hundred fifty people—tourists, schoolchildren, photographers, and geologists—going across the bridge just to look at the area. With the hundred dollars, I'd build a tollgate and charge one dollar a head. According to my calculations, you could net $1,273,000 during the next five years. If you add a concession for T-shirts and film, you could possibly add another $2.5 million."

That story captures the essence of my fifth principle, Profitable Attitude/Profitable Action. Her "eye" for opportunity was instinctive, but it can also be acquired. In this chapter, you'll learn the elements that comprise a profitable attitude and how to develop those same traits. And you'll also learn how to rid yourself of profit-blockers, the self-limiting mental attitudes that destroy the possibility of success before you ever begin.

THE PROFIT BLOCKERS

In moneymaking, as in nearly every other area of life, we fall into certain patterns of behavior that can subtly but powerfully limit our potential. Here are nine profit-blocking attitudes that can keep you from achieving all you are capable of:

1. The Mañana Syndrome

The motto of the Mañana Syndrome is, "I'll get to it tomorrow," whether the topic is paying the bills, balancing the checkbook, keeping track of receipts, checking out an insurance policy, or having a will made out.

Procrastinators in the money field are like procrastinators in every other aspect of life. They choose to live in a fantasy world, waiting and hoping that something will happen to tie up the loose ends. But it never does.

If you're a procrastinator, the best advice I can give you is to hire someone to handle the routine, money-related details in your life so you can apply your energy more productively to other areas. Handing your bills to your accountant each month can free you from the hassle and give you more time for making money. Yes, you *can* afford to do so—and you'll be rid of the guilt and the inconvenience. Procrastination is a childish form of control that really only leaves you in a weaker position. But, of course, procrastinators already know that.

2. The Assumers

People with this profit-blocker assume that someone else—husband, wife, lover, parents, employer, trust officer—is going to take responsibility for their financial success.

A classic example of this habit was unwittingly exhibited by a husband and wife I interviewed separately for a segment on money attitudes for "The Today Show" several years ago.

First I interviewed the wife and asked how she felt about the economy, which was then in dreadful shape.

"I'm very concerned," she said. "I've certainly seen things in better condition."

"How do you feel about your personal finances?" I asked.

"On that score I feel much more confident because my husband is a financial genius. He watches over our business affairs and I know he's taking good care of everything."

Then I interviewed the husband.

"How do you feel about today's economy?" I asked.

"Things look pretty bad. In fact, I haven't seen things look this dismal in nearly fifty years."

"How do you feel about your own personal finances?"

"I feel pretty comfortable in that area because my wife is a whiz when it comes to managing our money. She makes sure that our investments are handled properly. I don't know what we'd do if she weren't so good with money."

Both were Assumers without even realizing it.

Another case of assuming that everything was taken care of was chronicled in the best-selling book *Widow*, written by Lynn Caine, who documents her experiences when her husband died of cancer—including her feeling of helplessness when she discovered the horrible financial state she was in. She had always believed the family finances were well managed because, after all, her husband was an attorney. After his death, however, she discovered that everything was a mess, and he didn't even have life insurance. She was stuck with the responsibility of raising her two children with no money. She was an Assumer whose world fell apart until she learned to take responsibility for her financial welfare.

There is an old adage—"Assume nothing." It's particularly applicable in regard to money.

3. The Passive Players

"I'm really not interested in financial details because I find money quite boring," says the Passive Player. A rich countess can use that line until she's about twenty-two; for anyone else, it's not only tedious, it's costly. Can you afford to be uninformed about what's happening with your money? I doubt it.

4. The Spenders

Most Spenders have a walletful of credit cards they use with the philosophy, "Live for today, to hell with tomorrow!"

Spenders make a good salary, live well, and have few debts, but they have nothing put away for the future—or even for next week. This attitude assumes a certain omnipotence—"I'll be fine forever"—as well as a certain childlike quality. It is, however, a game that can be costly in terms of wasted profit-potential.

My advice to Spenders is to activate a payroll savings deduction plan where you work or a similar plan where you bank. If you're honest with yourself, you'll admit that you usually spend all that's available each month. If less is available, you'll get used to spending less, and you'll also be building a nest egg that can give you future security or serve as the basis for eventual investments.

5. Cliff-Hangers

You can see these folks in the McDonald's television commercials where the youthful customer laments having only $2 until payday. Cliff-Hangers make a habit of living on the edge, month in and month out. They're the ones who habitually ask, "Can you lend me a few bucks until I get paid?" They never have quite enough to make ends meet, and certainly never have enough for the extra things they really want.

Cliff-hanging isn't limited to twenty-one-year-olds in McDonald's ads; it can be found among people at all levels of the economic ladder, including many senior executives. A top television producer once told me that he runs short about once a month and cures the problem by doing some filming on location. Why does he go on location? So that he can get a cash advance to tide him over until payday.

If that ploy rings a bell, you know you're not alone. But also know that you can change this behavior, because it certainly isn't part of a Profitable Attitude. Even if they're occasionally caught short, people with a Profitable Attitude have an overdraft account—or line of credit with the bank. They know that running short from time to time can happen to anyone, but doing it repeatedly is quite another thing.

6. The Blamers

The Blamers put the responsibility for their financial failure on the shoulders of someone else. "If only they hadn't spent all the money," or, "If only they hadn't invested in that deal that went sour, we'd be set now," they say. Quite often the culprit is seen to be an ex-wife or ex-husband.

The best advice I can give Blamers is to cut your ties with past losses and recognize the futility in blaming anyone else for your problems. Back to basics once again: *You are responsible for your financial situation.* That situation can change—and it can *be* changed. But you're the only person who can make it happen.

If you're a Blamer, you might find it helpful to write out your resentments, make lists of the people you blame for your situation, then dispose of what you have written. The method by which you stop blaming is not as important as the fact that you end the blaming habit.

Another way to short-circuit the blaming process is to take action right now in an area in which you've been blaming someone else for your failure. If you've blamed someone—a spouse or an employer—for not providing you with insurance coverage, call an agent yourself and make arrangements to buy a policy. If you've blamed someone for not selling a stock that has cost you money, call your broker and take care of the matter yourself. Taking action is the most significant part of stopping the blaming process, and it'll allow you to cut a new path for the future.

7. The Talkers

The Talkers' motto is, "Quote all the latest financial deals and statistics—but don't actually *do* anything."

The Talkers are the sidewalk economists, the financial weather-reporters. To listen to them, you'd think they were making bundles of money, since they're obviously so well informed. But, as I've found out over the years, there is no correlation between knowledge and net worth unless that knowledge is backed by action.

Ironically, the professional field with the most Talkers is the financial services business, which includes lawyers and CPAs—and heads of financial institutions.

If you've been concerned about your knowledge quotient vs. your net worth, this is a good time to examine the reasons for that concern. Talking is often a great means of avoiding responsibility for your own financial future. By the time you read Chapter 9, HALT: High Action/Low Talk, you'll see how to put that knowledge to profitable use.

8. The Victims

Seeing yourself as a Victim can either be a temporary response to a specific situation or a life-long modus operandi.

Anyone can feel like a Victim from time to time, but if you find that everything you touch turns into a bad investment, or if you always end up on the wrong end of a financial deal, you might want to ask yourself why that's happening. If you discover that you're being victimized as a way of life, you might be wise to seek professional psychological help, because chronic victims usually find that their point of view pervades all aspects of their life.

Whether you realize it or not, you write your own life script. You are also the director and producer of that script. You *can* change and edit the scripts to come out the way you want them to. You can become the victor instead of the victim.

9. The Poor-Mouthers

"I don't have enough money to take a vacation."

"I can't go out to dinner until payday."

"I'd love to, but I really can't afford it. You know how expensive everything is."

Those are just some of the standard phrases you'll hear from the Poor-mouthers, who are close cousins to the Blamers and closer cousins to the Victims.

126

Poor-mouthing is more often a state of mind than a reflection of reality. A friend of mine was married to a man who was always poor-mouthing. For more than ten years she tried to get him to see the bountiful part of life and accept the fact that he could afford a lovely home in a first-rate neighborhood. The man was a millionaire several times over. She finally stopped trying to convince him to change. She now lives in the style she wants—and he does, too, in another city with other people.

WHAT IS A PROFITABLE ATTITUDE?

Your attitude can be one of your strongest assets or one of your biggest handicaps when dealing in the money world. Your attitude is based on all the things you've learned and experienced over the years, including myths, facts, fiction—even the excuses you've dreamed up. It reflects millions, if not billions, of inputs you've received throughout your life.

People with a Profitable Attitude have a certain way of looking at the world and the financial opportunities it presents. They have faith in their moneymaking ability and take responsibility for their own financial success. They're living proof of that old adage that being poor—or rich—is largely a state of mind. One way to acquire that attitude is to let go of the money myths that cripple your profit potential. For example:

Myth: You Have to Have Money to Make Money

Fact: While the Rockefellers, Mellons, and Fords might have a head start in the money game because of their inherited wealth, there are many, many rich people who have made their own fortunes. In fact, many extremely successful people in this country—including Jerry Buss, real estate tycoon and owner of the Los Angeles Lakers and Kings sports teams; the late Ray Kroc, founder of the McDonald's empire; and Jeno Paulucci, the man behind Jeno's Pizza—started with *no money* and *no influential family connections.*

The important thing is not how much money you're born with, but what you learn along the way about making more than you have. For example, the moneymaking package I developed for the Post Office manager from Salt Lake City didn't cost her a dime. It did, however, require an expenditure of her time and expertise, which we matched with my own. Most of the people you've met in this book started out with modest financial resources—and all of them managed to achieve financial success.

Remember, you don't have to *have* money to make money—you just have to have *access* to money. In other words, you have to know *where* and *how* to borrow money you can use to leverage yourself into making deals. (Leverage is a small amount of money controlling a larger amount of money or the equivalent of a larger amount of money. You put, say, 20 percent down on the condo, borrow 80 percent, and control 100 percent of a condo-rental business. Once you understand the basic concept of leverage, you can see how it can be applied in business situations, such as the now-famous leverage buy-outs in real estate deals, or in everyday situations such as purchasing a car.)

In my last book, *Where to Get Money for Everything*, I explained how to get money for a variety of purposes. In that book I told how you can apply the use of leverage to getting a college education (through the use of student loans and the student aid program), to real estate, to starting a company and to making most kinds of investments. I also discussed how leverage can even be used in the stock market, where its classic use is the margin account, which allows you to take control of a stock by paying a percentage of its face value. A note of caution, however: In all of these situations, your leverage is based upon your ability to prove that you *can* and *will* pay the money back.

Whenever you find yourself making the excuse that you need money to make money, remind yourself that capital is available to more people today than at any other time in history. In the past, significant sums were available only to the likes of the Mellons, the Carnegies, and the Rothschilds. Today it's not uncommon for the average person to have ten credit cards in his or her wallet. When you total up the credit lines available on each of those ten credit cards, you see how much money you really have access to.

Myth: You Have to Be Good With Numbers to Be Financially Successful

Fact: I often hear from men and women alike, "How can I be successful in the money world when I can't even balance my checkbook?" I always point out that balancing a checkbook is essentially a function of the logical, linear, left hemisphere of the brain, while making money utilizes the creative, conceptual, right side of the brain—the side that functions in making real estate deals, spotting investment opportunities, or creating potential moneymaking blockbusters such as the Pet Rock, Kentucky Fried Chicken, and the McDonald's hamburger empire. Insight is fundamental to moneymaking genius—ability with numbers comes into play only after the conceptual or creative action has already taken place. (Besides, once you make money, you can always hire someone to keep track of your checkbook!)

When Thomas Edison created his inventions, he wasn't calculating the price-earnings ratio of Edison Company stock. First came the concept, the invention, the observation that would ultimately light up our lives. It wasn't until twenty years later that the Edison Company became publicly traded and the numbers became part of the process.

130

Myth: You Have to Have a Harvard MBA or Be Trained as an Economist to Be Successful With Money

Fact: Take a closer look at the backgrounds of some of the most fabulously wealthy men and women in this country and you'll find most of them *never even attended college.* Bill Lear of LearJet, Ray Kroc of McDonald's and Jeno Paulucci of Jeno's Pizza and their ilk didn't learn their craft on ivy-covered campuses.

It's an illusion that making money requires sophisticated knowledge enjoyed only by those with highly specialized degrees. In fact, I believe there are probably more millionaires who *don't* have degrees than there are who do.

The knowledge that *is* necessary for making money falls into a formula that I call CAT:

C = Curiosity, to do research, to check out what you learn;

A = Action, to begin to take steps to bring your observations into a workable form;

T = Thought, to proceed with common sense.

I also have developed what I call Nelson's Law: *We learn by doing.* I urge you to look at this method of self-education, not as Trial and Error, but as Trial and Learn. Trying and doing are still the best ways I know of to learn about making money.

If you have a Harvard MBA or a degree in economics, you *do* have a wonderful store of knowledge—but you don't necessarily have a moneymaking advantage over anyone else. It all depends on how you are able to use that knowledge, doesn't it?

Myth: You Have to Know the Language of the Money World Before You Can Function in the Money Arena

Fact: It really isn't that important to know the money lingo of Wall Street. While the money world has a language all of its own—basis points, T-Bills, M1, short-term, sell short, etc.—it's more essential to understand the *concepts* than to know the words that describe them. And most important is being able to spot an investment opportunity based on your own observations and experience. Remember Susan Reynolds and the Kentucky Fried Chicken? She knew little about stock market terminology, but she trusted her instincts.

If you really want to learn the money world's language, you can visit your local library or bookstore and pick up a few basic primers, such as the ones I list in Chapter 9. If you're interested in a specific investment area, you'll probably find out everything you need to know with the assistance of a few good books as you go along.

For example, several years ago a friend of mine was going through a complicated real estate deal under the guidance of her attorney. Even though she considered herself a novice in the real estate field, I noticed that each time we talked, she peppered her conversation with increasingly elaborate details concerning "wraparound mortgages," "1033 exchanges," and a host of other tax- and finance-related real estate activities.

One day I stopped her in midsentence and said, "You might not realize it, but you've become a real estate expert—you even talk like one!" She was surprised at my observation until she realized that she had indeed become knowledgeable by going through the process required to complete her deal. By attending the meetings with her attorney, listening to the conversations, participating in the strategizing, and being involved in carrying the deal through to completion, she had learned more than she ever could have picked up by reading *The Wall Street Journal* every day of her life. She had unwittingly received a crash course in real estate, including all the jargon to go with it.

Myth: All the Big Moneymaking Opportunities Are Gone

Fact: Economic opportunities are more available today than ever before in history, as evidenced by the fact that 1 out of every 400 people in this country is a millionaire. And it is easier than ever to make serious money, since the primary qualifications for success are *information* and *expertise*, not capital. In his fine book *Megatrends*, John Naisbitt says that this country's change from an industrial to an informational society has brought a wealth of opportunities for those who understand the value of their knowledge and expertise. A clear indication

133

of this trend is the number of service industries that have sprung up in the past ten years. Businesses that sell information are now in the economic forefront.

A PROFITABLE ATTITUDE IS:

• Knowing that you have a right to make as much money as you want to;

• Understanding that the only limits on your income are your own perception of your value and the marketplace's perception of your value;

• Having a clear understanding of your rights, including your right to say "No" and "I don't understand";

• Realizing that you can reject, as well as accept, opportunities that come your way;

• Knowing that an opportunity that's too good to be true is usually just that;

• Being aware that there's money to be made in every financial climate, whether the country is in the middle of a recession or enjoying prosperity;

• Understanding that mistakes are the tuition of the money world. (It's impossible to get a college education for free, so why should you expect to learn about moneymaking without losing a dime? Think of your acceptable losses as an investment in learning about moneymaking);

• Feeling good about the financial success of others;

• Feeling confident about your ability to make money;

• Being self-protective and refusing to be put in situations in which you'll get taken advantage of;

• Having a well-balanced attitude about money and moneymaking and striving for balance between work and play in your life.

TRANSLATING PROFITABLE ATTITUDES INTO PROFITABLE ACTION

Once you begin to nurture a Profitable Attitude, you'll find that Profitable Action will become an automatic extension of your new way of looking at the world around you. Thinking and attitude alone, however, will not make you successful—or rich. Opportunities are there, but you must pursue them and make them happen through Profitable Action.

WHAT IS PROFITABLE ACTION?

• Using leverage—that is, becoming proficient in the art of using someone else's money to achieve your goals;

• Paying yourself first—having a savings plan and sticking to it, no matter how tempted you might be by the sale at the local boutique;

• Taking risks—*and* knowing how to maximize your chance of success and minimize the potential of failure (you'll learn how in Chapter 7, Risk Taking/Reward Getting);

• Setting long- and short-range financial goals for yourself;

• Keeping current on financial trends and other relevant information;

• Negotiating when and where necessary—and doing your homework to make certain you have the best possible odds of achieving the result you want;

• Contributing your time, money, and expertise to others, realizing that you have to give in order to get;

• Asking smart questions and taking quality advice;

• Automating, delegating, creating, and affiliating to put yourself in a Position to Profit;

• Jumping in and making an offer when a good opportunity arises, even though you realize that your offer might not be accepted;

• Knowing how to get out of any deal before you decide to get into it;

• Getting the details of a deal in writing;

• Using your local shopping malls as an economic indicator, realizing that there's an important message about the economy whenever you see people walking around a mall without packages under their arm;

136

- Assuming nothing—getting the facts;
- Becoming an "instant expert" on topics that are relevant to you, using the local library or bookstore to your advantage;
- Picking a money adviser as you would a dentist, minimizing the potential for pain;
- Going with informed hunches;
- Changing when times change;
- Recognizing winners in people, products, stocks, and deals—and always going with a winner;
- Surrounding yourself with a network of smart people and financial-service professionals;
- Watching fads, but investing only in trends.

CHAPTER 7

Risk Taking/Reward Getting

You have to take risks if you want to make money, which is probably one of the major reasons why so many people stay in their financial rut. That's a shame, because there's no other area of life in which risks are as controllable and as manageable as they are in the financial area—if you know what you're doing.

Successful risk-taking is merely another part of the process of making serious money—and it, too, can be learned. In this chapter you'll see how to become comfortable with various levels of risk, how to create a Risk Safety Net, and how to develop your own Risk Comfort Zone so you can stop being intimidated by what you consider to be the hazards of moneymaking and get on with the process of making serious money.

Diana Zankan is a woman who's not afraid to

take intelligent risks—and she usually ends up accomplishing what she sets out to do. When I met her several years ago, her divorce had just turned final, the ink on her realtor's license was barely dry, and she had had it with apartment living.

She wanted to buy a house, but knew she had little in the way of traditional assets—she was new at her job and could show hardly any savings. Because she had just completed studying for her realtor's license exam, however, she also knew what bankers look for in prospective borrowers: the Three Cs of Credit, which are Character, Capital, and Capacity. (In other words, *Do* you pay? *Can* you pay? and *Will* you pay?) Since she had lived her whole life in one community, attended school and college there, and been a member of numerous social and business clubs, she decided she *did* have a strong asset in banker's terms after all—her very impressive contacts with business and community leaders through her life long participation in everything from the Girl Scouts to the Chamber of Commerce.

She went shopping for a house, found one she loved, and made an appointment to talk to the president of her local bank to see about the possibility of getting a loan. She was well prepared for the interview and presented him with verification of her status as a solid member of the community, complete with a statement of anticipated earnings from her new employer and many glowing letters of reference from highly placed business and community people who vouched for her character and industriousness. Several of them even offered to serve as her cosigners.

Her proposal was unorthodox to say the least. But her tenacity, positive attitude, and overall character so impressed the bank president that he agreed to consider her application.

She heard nothing for a month, and then when she had nearly given up hope that her loan would be approved, she received a call from her banker, saying that they'd agreed to approve her application, unusual as it was.

Diana told me her story when I was doing research for a television segment on women and real estate. I listened to her story in amazement, then asked, "But what if the bank had turned you down? Weren't you taking an incredible risk?"

"Not really," she said with a shrug. "There must have been at least fifty other banks in town. I'd have kept trying until I found one that was willing to take a chance on me. I knew that the house I'd chosen was a valuable piece of real estate, which meant the money would be well secured for the bank that did decide to take a chance on me. It was just a matter of time until I found a bank that saw the situation the same way I did."

Diana's attitude exemplifies what I mean by my sixth principle, Risk Taking/Reward Getting. She knew that the only way she could get what she wanted was by taking a chance, so that's what she did. She wasn't afraid to hear "no" over and over again because she was confident that eventually she'd hear "yes."

Susan Morton-Daniels talks of the major experience she had with risk taking when she decided to branch out on her own in the consulting/training business. A corporate expert on affirmative action programs in the late 1970s, she considered offering her expertise to a number of companies on a consultancy basis.

"It always sounds good to go off and do your own thing. But when you're the only parent of a five-year-old and have a mortgage, the risk is high. When I made my decision to launch my own consulting business, I lined up contracts in advance of leaving my job to soften the risk. I already had half a dozen contracts the day I walked out the door, but the question was 'Will there be more contracts after those initial six?' Corny as it seems, my other question was 'Will I be able to feed my child?'"

Nine years later, with a firm that now employs ten and also offers corporate strategic planning and research services, the answer is clearly "yes."

Maria Ferrare faced a dilemma following her divorce five years ago—she could go to work for $4 an hour as an untrained office worker or she could take the risk of starting her own company. The thought of working for peanuts so motivated her that she set about turning herself into an expert on Italian delis. She spent four months checking out gourmet food operations, tracking down distributors and wholesalers, investigating storefront locations, and studying customer traffic patterns to pick the best spot for her own deli. She met with a banker who took her through the necessary elements of putting together a business plan. She ended up rewriting the plan four times before the banker finally granted her a $125,000 loan with her house as security.

That was the moment of truth. She had just enough money for six months' worth of inventory, rent, and salaries. If her deli didn't make it, she was running the risk of failing in her own business venture—*and* losing her home.

"It was a huge risk—one I might not take today," she says. But luck was with her. Not only did the upscale location she selected turn out to be perfect for attracting the Italian deli crowd, but her catering business also grew rapidly. Her only problem after her first three months was finding a larger location in the same neighborhood for her business.

An even more dramatic story is that of Jim Davidson, a merchandising expert for a manufacturing company, who was presented with a unique career option when he was offered a job with a group that had been assembled to work on a special four-year project. He would have to take a pay cut of $15,000 a year, even though he'd essentially be doing the same kind of work he was already involved in. He wouldn't see a payoff on his efforts for the entire four years—and even then there was some doubt about whether the situation would be a success or a failure. He decided to take the risk— and become one of the original team members of a group called the 1984 Los Angeles Olympic Organizing Committee. His payoff was participation in an outstanding accomplishment—and carte blanche with just about any major corporation he might now be interested in joining.

THE FOUR FACTORS OF THE RISK GAME

One of the ways to get more comfortable with risk taking is to realize that the same four factors are at work in any risk situation—whether it's riding your first two-wheeler, skydiving, launching a new company, choosing a money market fund, or buying your first home.

1. The Self Factor

How confident are you about your knowledge and skills in this area? Are you an experienced investor, or a neophyte who'll have to depend totally upon the recommendations of your advisers? Do you have good reason to trust your judgment or are you whistling in the dark? Your degree of expertise, knowledge, and confidence needs to be evaluated here.

2. The Other-People Factor

Whether the other people involved in a deal are attorneys, bankers, CPAs, business partners, or investors, you need to evaluate their track record, reputation, motivation, trustworthiness, and over-

144

all compatibility with your goals, strengths, and weaknesses.

3. The Outside Factor

Like life itself, investments and other business deals are affected by what insurance companies call "acts of God"—accidents, deaths, the weather, and so on. For example, fortunes have been made and lost in rubber crops because of variations in rainfall patterns. In evaluating this factor, you need to determine to what degree the success or failure of your endeavor will be affected by forces over which you have little or no control. Your key to long-term success will be your ability to anticipate as many problems as possible, develop ways to turn them around to your advantage, and bail out if and when it looks like you're in a no-win situation.

4. The Information/Access Factor

The entire financial world is based upon access to information—he/she who has timely information can profit. Where do you fit into the information pipeline? Do you have to wait to get news about a new company from your broker, who gets it from the wire service, which gets it from the company's public relations agency? Then you might be in trouble. Even worse, are you attempting to monitor your stock investments with information that comes out on a weekly rather than a daily—or hourly—basis? If you're in an investment field that's highly sensitive to split-second information, and you don't have access to that information, you might as well save your money and get out now.

Walking through the following example will give you a feeling for how to use your awareness of those four factors when evaluating risk situations, even those as out of the ordinary as skydiving.

> *Situation:* Skydiving
>
> *Self Factor:* Your ability, experience, and confidence level
>
> *Other-People Factor:* The skill of the pilot and other vital members of the support team
>
> *Outside Factor:* The weather, wind conditions, condition of the parachute, amount of air traffic over the jump site
>
> *Information/Access Factor:* Data about the topography of the jump site, pilot's track record, weather forecasts, technical instructions

Even though the thought of skydiving might send chills up your spine, as it does mine, you can see how breaking the risk situation down into those four factors gives you a framework for evaluating the situation on an objective basis. The very evaluation process itself may give you a feeling of confidence, of being in control, which then carries over into the risk situation itself.

CREATING YOUR RISK SAFETY NET

Using the following five pointers to create what I call a Risk Safety Net can also significantly minimize the sense of impending danger you might feel in risk situations.

1. Never Go Into a Deal Unless You Know Your Way Out

This is one of my cardinal rules for any type of risk taking, whether it involves negotiating a raise, making an investment decision, or buying a home. The more you know about the ins and outs of the deal, the better able you'll be to deal with any anxiety you feel about your decision. First, you need to determine your downside risk by evaluating what you consider to be the worst thing that could possibly happen in the situation, then you need to decide how you'd deal with that scenario.

Let's take, for example, buying your first home. You locate a house, discover that you have enough for the down payment, and begin to ask yourself the uncomfortable questions: What if something happens and I can't make the payments, cover the taxes, or handle the overall financial responsibility?

147

The downside risk—the worst that could happen—would be losing the house and the money you've already invested in it. But there is a wide range of options you could pursue that would allow you to land on your feet, even under that scenario.

• You could sell the house and recover the money you've already put into it.

• You could turn your purchase into a team investment and bring in several other investors who could help you swing the payments.

• You could rent the house out and use the rental payments to help cover the mortgage.

In the stock market, you can maximize your options and minimize your losses by placing what's called a sell order on the stock at the time of purchase. Once you select a stock and make a purchase, you simply instruct your broker to sell if the stock drops below a certain price. The minute the stock drops to that level, it goes on the sale block, protecting your "going-in" price, as well as your downside risk. For example, in his excellent book *Battle for Investment Survival*, Gerald Loeb advises selling a $30 stock the minute it drops to 29.

So even if the worst that could happen did occur in either the home-buying or the stock-market situation, you'd still have options you could pursue to salvage your investment. There are usually as many alternatives for getting out of a risk situation as there are for getting into it. Realizing this fact should go a long way toward relieving risk-related anxiety.

A word of caution here, however. Although the

sell order tactic works fine when trading Blue Chips and other major stocks that have plenty of potential buyers, it won't do much good to put a sell order on a stock that nobody wants to buy. For example, Over-the-Counter stocks are new issues that generally have what's called a limited market. It's more difficult to find buyers when the stock you're offering appeals only to a small arena of potential investors.

One way to get a rough idea of whether a company's stock has limited appeal is by checking to see how broad its base of support is. If there are 100,000 stockholders, you're in relatively good shape, because you know that there are 99,999 other people out there who are interested in the stock and who'd be potential buyers if you decide to sell. If, on the other hand, there are only 5,000 stockholders, your attempts to sell your stock would depend upon appealing to members of a much more limited market. In other words, a Blue Chip stock has far greater liquidity than an Over-the-Counter issue because it's much easier to sell if you should decide to do so.

You should also be aware that investments in a business, real estate, diamonds, art, antiques, and silver are far less liquid than those in the stock market because:

• There's no "established market" as there is on the floor of the Wall Street brokerage houses.

• You may or may not find a buyer who's interested in what you want to sell.

• There is a fairly lengthy selling process.

149

• The value is based upon somewhat subjective criteria, reflecting supply and demand and the whim of the marketplace.

And there might be legal and/or contractual considerations as well. In a real estate limited partnership or shared equity arrangement, for example, there could be a number of contractual stipulations that will have an impact on how quickly you can walk away with your money if you decide to get out of the deal. There might be provisions in the partnership contract that limit your resale to the other general partners, who can buy back your interest for your original purchase price or fair market value. Or your partners might have the right to approve or disapprove of the potential buyer you have lined up. If you're considering involvement in a shared equity situation, be sure to check the contract to find out what limitations it imposes on your ability to get out of the deal.

2. Know Your Options

Few financial risks involve all-or-nothing situations with only one route to the payoff. You might have to try a variety of strategies before you find the one that works.

When you're thinking about a bank loan, for example, it's important to realize that even if you get turned down, there are other money sources you can approach to achieve the outcome you want. (See Chapter 5, NCR: No Cash Required.) The more you understand the subtleties of the lending world, the more you'll see how many and not how few options you have.

3. Do Your Homework

The more prepared you are, the better your chance of success will be in any financial risk situation. Whether you're buying a home, asking for a bank loan, investing in a franchise, or going after a raise, you'll find that doing your homework will have a direct impact on the outcome of the situation.

Take the bank loan, for example. Doing your homework would involve the following steps:

• *Making sure you're approaching the right banker.* All banks—and bankers—are not alike. Some specialize in serving small businesses, others tailor their services to big corporations, while still others try to woo the small investor. If you don't fit a bank's very specific preferred-client profile, you'll probably never get more from the relationship than a safe place to keep your money.

Before applying for a loan, size up the bank you're dealing with. What message do they espouse in their advertisements, and what feeling do you get from the vice president you deal with? If you're currently running a small company, you'll probably get top-drawer treatment from the business and entrepreneurial banks, but you may well be ignored by a large "retail" bank, which is primarily interested in meeting the specialized needs of the average employed person with a paycheck.

Ask your accountant to recommend a bank that's likely to be a good match for you.

• *Getting an Introduction.* Lining up the right bank is a lot like meeting the right people: The best way is through an introduction. Since all accountants work closely with local financial institutions, ask yours for a personal introduction—either by phone or letter—to the vice president of the bank most likely to treat you as an important customer. That introduction will give you clout for one simple reason: Accountants have many clients who not only need loans, but also have significant sums to deposit. Banks, therefore, like to stay in favor with accountants, who can refer many new customers their way.

• *Knowing the Details of Your Credit Report.* Even though bankers can make a loan based solely on their own personal judgment (this is called signatory capacity), they seldom bypass credit reports when deciding whether to approve or reject a loan application. Because it has such a strong bearing on the attractiveness of your application, it's important for you to know what's included in your credit report before you meet with your banker. To obtain a copy of your record, contact TRW and Commercial Credit, which are both listed in your local telephone directory. For a small fee (usually from $4 to $7), they'll send you a copy of your report, which you can review for errors, inaccuracies, and negative information.

• *Offsetting Negative Information and Setting the*

Record Straight. Credit records are not always accurate. In fact, TRW admits that they probably list incorrect information for as many as 2 percent of the names they have on file.

If you're among that 2 percent, it is your responsibility to spot the inaccuracy and *your* responsibility to get it corrected. You should take two actions: Contact the creditor who reported the incorrect information. Then submit your side of the situation to the credit reporting agency. It doesn't end there. Keep track of the situation until you see the accurate information on your report.

If there is accurate information that reflects badly on your credit-worthiness, your only option is to be honest and explain to your banker how and why you fell behind in your payment obligations. If you were going through a divorce, suffered a death in the family, had a job transfer, or were ill, discuss how it affected your credit and how that situation has been handled. Remember, don't try to hide negative information—confront it honestly and then counter it with good news about the responsible way in which your finances are now being handled.

• *Letting Your Banker Know Who You Are.* Bankers are in the people business—they're eager to meet you and have you as a customer. They know they're facing increased competition, not only from other banks and savings and loans, but also from insurance companies and brokerage firms that have entered the financial services field. Use this fact to your advantage and make sure your banker knows, not only about your business affiliations, but about

153

your charity, community, and social affiliations as well. Bankers know that Girl Scouts U.S.A., for example, have large accounts they deposit in financial institutions. If you're a Girl Scout troop leader, let your banker know about your involvement.

• *Taking Advantage of Corporate Clout.* You probably have more economic clout at your bank than you think.

A Los Angeles woman who's the accountant for a group of Beverly Hills doctors recently told me she was having trouble getting a $10,000 loan from her bank.

"Do they know who you are?" I asked.

"Oh, yes, I've had an account there for years."

That wasn't what I meant. An accountant for five doctors carries a lot of weight—the equivalent of $1.5 million in potential deposits, in her case. I suggested that she rethink her approach and talk to her bank again—not as an individual, but as the person who controls her own assets plus those of very successful, high-deposit doctors. She got the loan—and now is treated like a VIP by her bank.

The same principle applies if you work for a large company, since banks with big-business customers want to keep all their client's employees happy. Try the piggyback approach and bank with the institution your company banks with. You'll find that your affiliation with a major depositor works wonders in giving you clout with your banker.

• *Knowing Your Loan-Getting Strengths.* Loan granting is based on the Three Cs of Credit: Character, Capital, and Capacity which, as I said earlier, means, Can you pay? Do you pay? Will you pay? You need to determine which of the three is your strongest asset and then capitalize on it. Remember Diana Zankan, whose character got her loan? Being a good judge of character is an art—and it's also the number one qualification for being a good banker.

• *Businesslike Behavior Is Best.* If you have a question about how to dress for a meeting with the bank, go for the safe and sure route. I always dress for bank meetings as though I were going to a board of directors meeting. The point is to show that you mean business.

• *Presenting a Loan Package, Not Just an Application.* Just like you, I don't like to be turned down for a business loan, so I make a point of being overly prepared and giving the bank more information than they expect. You should do the same thing. Complete the application and then include a writeup similar to a résumé that gives a fuller overview of your career. If you have a new venture, be sure to include a complete business plan telling what you expect the company to achieve during the next eighteen months, as well as an explanation of how the loan is going to be used.

If the loan is for real estate, include a complete description of the property, including a photograph, if possible.

If you have letters of reference or any other written materials about yourself or the venture, include them in the package. (See the Appendix for a business plan outline.)

You may feel that this is too much like the "show

and tell" exercises of your youth. In a way, it is. But it's also a tried and true method to help you get the loan. Walking in with a complete loan package can cause your banker to go into a brief state of professional shock, which gives you the advantage in that situation.

• *Making a List of Your Other Loan-Getting Options Before You Go After the First One on Your List.* Listing your options helps defuse any sense of desperation you might have and takes away the "either/or" pressure. Realize that if you don't get the loan with this bank, then you'll get it with another bank. The confidence of knowing that there are other money sources can even result in a Mona Lisa smile instead of butterflies in the stomach.

ASKING FOR A RAISE

Doing your homework also makes sense in situations like asking for a raise. The smart person goes into the boss to bring up the issue of a raise after going on other job interviews, talking with job-placement headhunters, and making a list of other job opportunities to find out what the job market looks like. Without that knowledge, you really have no leverage. You might also be afraid that you will get turned down for the raise or be fired, and go to the meeting all too anxious. But careful preparation will arm you with confidence about your worth to your company and a realistic viewpoint of your value.

PREPARATION BEFORE ASKING FOR A RAISE

Ask yourself the following questions:

- Am I being fairly paid now?
- Is anyone in the company doing the same job and being paid substantially more than I am?
- Am I overdue for my raise?
- Can I justify in terms of contributions to the company why I should receive a raise?
- What would happen if I got turned down?
- Do I have other job opportunities and offers?
- Do I want more money, a new title, extra perks, more time off, more responsibility? (Be specific here.)
- Is my request for more money within the standard operating procedures of the company or am I asking for something out of the ordinary?
- Am I willing to keep my job at the current salary?
- What are the chances of being fired or creating bad blood by asking for a raise at this time?

Once the checklist has been completed, if you decide to go ahead, you can develop your presentation based on how well you know your boss and the political situation within the company. For instance, can your boss make the decision alone or will he/she need approval from others on high?

157

Will your boss need your request in writing or will your discussion be a basis for action? How far are you willing to push the situation?

How can you give yourself the ultimate safety net in this risk situation? By talking to some other firms or headhunters about jobs. Knowing you have options elsewhere will give you increased courage and confidence when you're sitting face to face with your boss.

Your safety net involves practical considerations as well. Try to hold your discussion out of your boss's office, away from the telephones and interruptions. Your office is ideal—if you have privacy. Or else schedule a lunch appointment to have the discussion.

QUESTIONS AFTER ASKING FOR THE RAISE

If the answer is affirmative, it's time to get the details on when the raise will go into effect. And be sure to express your appreciation!

QUESTIONS AFTER ASKING FOR THE RAISE IF THE ANSWER IS "SORRY"

This is the moment that you dreaded all along. But, even if the answer is "Sorry," you can keep the door open with a few important questions:

• Could you give me some more understanding of the current corporate financial problem?

• Are you requesting raises for the department in next year's budget?

158

• Is there a freeze on raises companywide or am I being singled out?

• Could you give me a time frame for discussing this in the next three to six months? Is that reasonable?

Listen for what's being said between the lines. Is this a nice way of telling you that you've reached your level of advancement there? Is your boss telling the truth or mollifying you?

4. Ask Probing Questions

Unfortunately, many people seem to think that asking questions means they're dumb. As long as you believe that, you can be intimidated into not asking important questions. (The simple truth is that money deals today are usually so complex that you *have* to ask questions in order to really understand the opportunity and the associated risk. Even professionals in the financial services field ask questions constantly. So should you.)

I made a fundamental mistake in this area when I neglected to ask several important questions going into a cattle-breeding tax shelter. I checked out the firm carefully before I made my $10,000 investment, but several months later I noted that the investment was already falling far short of my anticipated goal. I made a telephone call and learned that the herd was shrinking—cattle were

159

being lost in the severe winter weather. I hadn't thought of asking about that possibility! That lesson taught me to *always* ask about the worst-case scenario—what's the worst thing that can happen and what questions haven't I asked you that I should have?

5. Establish Your Risk Comfort Zone

You don't need to be miserable to make money. While I strongly encourage you to take reasonable risks even though you might be somewhat uncomfortable doing so in the beginning, I'll never tell you to put yourself in situations that cause you anxious, sleepless nights. Your own feelings—a sense of your Risk Comfort Zone—must be your guide. Remember, there are thousands of opportunities all around you—opportunities you can live with comfortably and profitably. You're the final judge of which moneymaking opportunities are right for you. *Listen to your instincts*, no matter what advice you might get from your accountant, attorney, friends, or relatives.

A woman at one of my seminars told me that her husband had once been involved in an investment situation that nearly wrecked their marriage. He had decided in 1979 to invest heavily in the gold market, which was particularly volatile at that time. The price of gold was changing so rapidly at various spots throughout the globe that he was setting the alarm clock each night to wake him several times between midnight and 6 A.M. so he could phone to get the latest closing prices at markets around the world. He became more and more obsessed with keeping constant track of his high-risk investment until his wife finally told him that he had to get out of the gold market—or get out, period. Because of her insistence, he liquidated his investment and managed to get out with a loss of "only" $2,000, which is quite a feat in a roller-coaster market situation like the one gold was in during the late '70s.

CHAPTER 8

PEP: Passion Equals Profit

Carole Ulrich Baer has an absolutely marvelous passion—playing games. She describes herself as "addicted" to games—card games, board games, any kind of games from gin rummy to pool. She's also fascinated with art—her background includes a degree in art and design, as well as professional experience with a commercial interior-design firm.

Carole combined these passions into a business success story that is anything but ordinary, building her newfound fortune on creation of an artistically designed, magnetic board game she calls **SPAZM**. The game has become a huge hit with the boutique crowd. It was licensed by the giant game-manufacturer Paragon-Reiss in 1983, and has been providing Carole with a steady and sizable income. She has also formed her own product development company, Beyond Boredom, Inc., which grossed close to a million dollars last year, and she's planning to go into the game-development consulting business.

The moral of that story is not the profit potential in game development or even the satisfaction of acquiring a fat net worth. Rather, the moral is the importance of *valuing your passion* and using it to improve your financial position, realizing that the most successful investment and moneymaking activities are those that reflect and build upon your own personality.

For example, at a recent gathering attended by a number of financially successful men and women, I realized that each person there had achieved his or her success through a different vehicle. One had become wealthy in real estate, another by starting her own stationery company. One had made money in the stock market, another through a venture capital deal, and still others had become successful through stamps, crafts, antiques, or collecting rare cars. The only common denominator to their moneymaking, I also realized, was the fact that each had used his or her own passion as the vehicle for success.

THE PASSION PROFIT TEST

While it's nearly impossible to get rich without it, passion can also lead you astray, for there are any number of things you might feel passionately about for which there is little economic value or return on investment.

For example, you might be thrilled about a particular artist, but you could also be the only one who feels that way. Go ahead and buy the artist's work if you like, but do so for pure enjoyment and not as part of your profit plan. Or you might feel passionately about property in Northern Canada, where only a caribou could survive. Buy an acre and build a summer cabin if you want, but don't kid yourself into thinking that you're going to make a profit on resale.

Whether you invest in paintings, stocks, antiques, old comic books, jade snuff bottles, or Ferraro T-shirts, the bottom line is simple: Can you make a profit? Passion can lead you to profit potential, but you'll also need your financial wisdom and *good judgment* to take you to the profit line.

Bob Simon has been in the stock market since his father gave him his first share of stock when he was fourteen, introducing him to an investment area that has become his life's great passion. Bob lives and breathes the stock market, and it has served as the basis for his now-considerable fortune.

His typical workday begins at 4:30 A.M., when he leaves his Marina del Rey condominium and drives to his brokerage office in downtown Los Angeles to research his pet stocks. He loves what he does, has a true sense of conviction about the market, and a feeling of excitement about the individual companies it represents. He ferrets out small, unknown firms like a modern Sherlock Holmes and then takes positions in their stocks, making appropriate recommendations to his clients. Bob was in the market when the Dow Jones was at 850, he was in when the Dow hit 1350, and he'll be in if it should go back down to 750. And whether the market itself is up or down, I have no doubt but that Bob will be making money. His passion for the market keeps him enthusiastic, involved, and active during the dull as well as the glamorous times. That passion has made him—and his clients—very successful.

Susan Kasen had a passion for beauty and design that manifested itself in her hobby of flower arranging. Living the comfortable life in South Orange, New Jersey, and married to a well-known music and book publisher, she decided about ten years ago that she wanted to do something more with her hobby than supplying her arrangements to local charities on a volunteer basis. She opened her own business and began doing stunning arrangements for local socialites' intimate parties. Before long she was handling entire banquets, weddings, and Bar Mitzvahs throughout New York and New Jersey. Her reputation soon grew to the point where she received a request from the late Princess Grace to attend Monaco's annual Flower Festival. Susan not only attended, but she did several of the arrangements for the most prestigious festival parties.

That exposure earned her an international reputation which was enhanced when the late Princess Grace sent her a personal note of thanks compli-

166

menting her on her artistic expertise. And it didn't hurt a bit when Monaco's Princess talked about Susan's talent to her friends in the White House. Soon afterward Susan opened The Green Thumb Florist in Manhattan. She now has Fortune 500 companies, the White House, and other notables among her clients.

Susan also followed her passion when it came time to invest the sizable profits she was making with her business. Although she looked into the stock market, real estate, and a variety of other investment possibilities, she was once again influenced by her passion for beauty and design and began to make some very wise art acquisitions. Her first major purchase was a painting by Lowell Nesbitt, who is known for his stunning irises. Susan now owns four of his works, a Botero and a Utaro. She has become a small but very successful art collector, and her passion has also brought her a great deal of enjoyment and satisfaction.

Harriet Epstein is a soap opera fanatic who found a way to build a new career out of her obsession. She was working for a department store chain in New Jersey in the public relations department several years ago when she was asked to arrange a series of publicity events, with celebrities making personal appearances. Since she loved the soaps so much—and wanted a chance to meet some daytime TV stars—she convinced her bosses to let her feature the soap performers at the events. The first of those happenings, which featured Ruth

Warrick of "All My Children," drew a phenomenal 2,300 people—and launched Harriet on a whole new career.

She began contacting other soap stars to appear in publicity events and did so well that she formed her own company, Soaps Alive!, which arranges appearances by TV performers at shopping centers, state fairs, and other events.

Harriet now runs offices in New Jersey, California, and Canada. Soaps Alive! is an extremely successful and profitable passion.

Fern Galant has a passion for traveling. That urge had only been partially satisfied by the occasional vacations she took with her husband and three children, so this New Jersey woman decided to start her own company, Grand Tours, which now offers elegant excursions to various cultural points of interest. Her clients rave about the first-class amenities she arranges, and she gets to travel to her heart's content.

University of Oregon student Phil Knight's passion was his hobby as a runner. He kept trying to run faster and better, and began to wonder if a different kind of running shoe might help him improve his performance on the track. He conferred with Bill Bowerman, the university's track coach, and they experimented until they designed the prototype for what eventually became the Nike line of running shoes.

Because I grew up in a Southern California family involved in building new homes and refurbishing old ones, I suppose it's only natural that I developed an early passion for real estate. As a child, I loved spending each weekend with my parents at various building sites, learning about real estate and the construction business by listening to them talk about what they were doing. It wasn't until I grew up and learned about economics, investments, and the use of leverage that I began to really understand why real estate is one of the finest investment vehicles around. And by then I was already hooked.

Mike Willard is an old friend of mine who handles relocation property appraisals for firms like IBM, Xerox, and Merrill Lynch. When you talk about real estate with Mike, you soon sense something special that sets him apart from others in his field—he loves what he's doing and it shows.

I recently asked Mike where he puts his personal investments. I wasn't the least bit surprised at his answer.

"I invest in real estate, of course. But while you'd probably think that my investments would be in large shopping malls, office buildings, and the like, that's not the case. I have a great affinity for single-family dwellings, so they've become the focus of my investment activities."

Mike went on to explain that his strategy involves investing in low-cost properties that are rented to vacationers in key resort areas around the country. None of his acquisitions are particularly plush, but all are beautifully decorated and maintained. And since he acquired them with three partners who are also real estate buffs, Mike's usual

169

investment is from $4,000 to $5,000 per property, allowing him to make the maximum profit on a minimum investment. He has a management company booking the rentals, and estimates that the resort homes are rented out for at least ten months a year.

When I asked him why he wasn't involved in more sophisticated, highly leveraged deals, he said, "This is what I know, it's what I feel comfortable with, and it has worked out very well for me."

Carlson Brothers Builders is a major apartment-complex development firm. It wasn't always such a glamorous operation, however. In the very beginning the construction company consisted of two brothers—a dentist and a real estate expert—who let their instincts and their passion guide them. The brothers would drive down a street, come to an area that looked interesting, and then one of them would say, "I think that corner over there is the right one to buy." They'd look at each other, agree, and go back to the office to have the papers drawn up. Their passion, their courage, and their wisdom have made them enormously successful. This seemingly intuitive approach was based on more than a decade of experience and lots of careful research.

Lane Nemeth is a woman who loves children. But, as the director of a Northern California day-care center and the mother of one young daughter, she was dismayed at the lack of quality educational toys she found in local toy stores. With $25,000 in backing from family and friends, in 1977 she began a small manufacturing enterprise, Discovery Toys, in the family garage. The company now has sales of nearly $20 million a year.

Chris Birchfield had always loved to sew. When she decided she was tired of trying to support herself and her young son by driving a school bus, she quit her job and began her own company making canvas handbags. Her last bus driver's paycheck just covered her supplies and office space rental, but within a short time she received enough orders for the reasonably priced bags to hire an assistant. Less than ten years later, Chris's company, Accessories Unlimited of Cornish, Maine, employs 100 people and boasts a multimillion-dollar sales profile.

Seventy-five-year-old Dora Stein has a similarly rewarding passion, but hers is for antiques. Even as a child, Dora had a lively curiosity about beautiful old things and began collecting all the information she could find about them. That early passion provided her with a solid background that helped her make wise choices when she started collecting the antiques themselves. To this day, she can walk into any junk store or posh antique shop and spot a well-priced Tiffany glass piece, an amber plate, a Queen Anne goblet, or a Louis XVI china pattern at twenty paces. Her trained eye has turned her into an active collector who is also profitably involved in buying and selling valuable pieces. Her antique collection, for which she probably paid a total of approximately $30,000 over the years, is now worth from $170,000 to $200,000, depending upon which pieces she has in her possession at any given time. Dora has also invested in stocks, bonds, and real estate from time to time, but nothing has given her the same emotional and financial rewards as her eye for antiques.

Dan Hillman, a successful California orthopedic surgeon, has a different eye—his is for vintage automobiles. While his primary investment vehicle has been prime Malibu waterfront property, he has also done quite well with his hobby of buying, restoring, and then reselling classic autos. His local mechanic lets him know when something interesting is available at a reasonable price. Then Dan goes to work, tinkering and fixing up his acquisitions. He enjoys the time he spends on the cars, which he resells for four to six times the price he pays for them.

Even in the area of tax shelters, my advice is to stick to vehicles that intrigue and attract you.

Several months ago I was being interviewed by the society editor of a large metropolitan newspaper. In our discussion, she mentioned that she was looking for a suitable tax shelter. As she asked me for my recommendations about oil, gas, real estate, and a variety of other shelters, I remembered that she had mentioned earlier how much she loved horses. I asked her to tell me more about that interest and learned that she had been involved in the equestrian world since she was a child. I told her that the best arrangement for her would be to invest in a horse-breeding tax shelter because she would have an advantage in that particular area based upon her own interest and enthusiasm.

172

On the other hand, the worst financial failures I've seen have taken place when people invested in areas in which they had no real interest or understanding. About ten years ago a friend of mine inherited a portfolio of stocks and bonds for which she had little enthusiasm. It never occurred to her to investigate any of them, to chart their ups and downs, or to take an active role in their management. Today the portfolio is worth approximately 25 percent of its value when she inherited it.

Her interest had always been in arts and antiques—she would have been better off selling the portfolio and investing the money in those areas. It turned out to be a very costly mismatch.

Tuning into your own investment personality is absolutely essential for financial success. Are you what I refer to as a "touch-and-feel investor"—that is, are you someone who is most comfortable investing in real estate, coins, art, or anything else that is tangible, that can be seen, touched, and felt? Or are you something of a gambler? Are you more interested in commodities and futures contracts than a slow, steady vehicle like stamps? Knowing and understanding your investment personality puts you ahead of the game, since the most successful investment strategies are those in which you are drawn to a specific investment vehicle. The more attractive and interesting the vehicle is to you, the more avidly you will follow that particular field, the more information you will acquire and process, the more likely you will be to stay well informed and aware as the trends ebb and flow.

173

Remember: Passion automatically sparks *curiosity*, which is perhaps the most vital ingredient of financial success. Curiosity is what causes you to get a copy of a company's quarterly or annual report before taking a look at investing in its stock. Curiosity is what leads you to ask questions about urban development and real estate trends, even when you're on vacation.

Curiosity is the basis of every successful investment endeavor and it is something you will have in abundance for those areas in which you have passionate interest.

CHAPTER 9

HALT: High Action/Low Talk

When you started reading this book, you probably wondered if it would really help you get rich. But now that you've come to the final chapter, I hope you've also come to the realization that there's only one factor that will really determine whether or not you make serious money—you.

So far I've told you how to see and evaluate the opportunities you already have all around you. I've shown you how to unblock your financial potential by rethinking, repackaging, and restructuring your moneymaking skills. I've demonstrated how to build your personal risk-taking safety net, how to profit from your passions, and how to get started with little or no cash outlay on your part.

But the most important principle in this book, the one that will ultimately determine whether or not you'll make serious money, involves the one thing I can't do for you—and that is to *take action*.

175

If you're like most people, you've read any number of how-to-be-a-success books. You've undoubtedly been inspired when you've finished them, but then you've put them away on the bookshelf and forgotten about them. I want this book to be different—and I want you to help me in making it so. This chapter is the dividing line between what you've done in the past and what you'll achieve in the future. And it will be your commitment to action that will make that difference.

So many of us avoid taking action because we're afraid that the course we've chosen won't lead to the results we want. That's why I'd like you to keep in mind that even after a commitment to action has been made, it can usually be terminated if the situation isn't turning out the way you'd like it to. Don't forget, I'm the one who believes in *cutting losses* before they get out of hand. You aren't locked into anything—unless you want to be.

As Steve Friedman, my former producer on "The Today Show," used to tell me when I felt anxious about a segment we were preparing, "Remember, Paula, it ain't brain surgery."

BEGIN WHERE YOU ARE TODAY

You don't have to be limited by what has happened in the past, nor do you have to correct every money mistake you've ever made in order to enjoy success

176

in the future. You only need to begin where you are at this very moment. Your enthusiasm and the new awareness you have gained about moneymaking opportunities and how to use them will help you to do just that.

Let's take some examples of financial situations you may be facing and examine courses of immediate action you can take to deal with them.

Situation: You want to start investing in the stock market.

Suggested Action: Jump in with both feet and make a small splash by buying one share of stock. It's the quickest, easiest way I know of to learn about investing in the stock market. If you're unsure about which stock to buy, you can choose a safe, solid Blue Chip like IBM, or you might even decide to buy a share of the company you're working for if it's publicly held. You might decide that you want to limit yourself to a stock that sells for less than $50—or even $25—a share. You certainly don't need a stockbroker's advice to buy one share of stock.

The point, of course, is to *make a commitment*, which means to take action. Once you're involved in the market, even on that small scale, you'll have the daily excitement of following your stock to see how it's doing. You'll find yourself reading the annual and quarterly reports of the company you've invested in, and you might even decide to attend the stockholders' annual meetings, which you'll have the right to do.

Many beginning investors try to learn about the

market by tap-dancing around the edges. They remind me of people who try to learn how to swim by reading a book. It simply can't be done! The best way to learn how to swim is to jump in the shallow end of the pool and get wet. It's the same thing with the stock market. Jump in, get wet, and start to swim! With one stock, you'll never sink—but you'll definitely learn more than you ever would by reading the latest investment books.

Another approach for the beginning investor is to become a member of an investment club. There are hundreds of investment clubs around the country, usually with from 50 to 200 members, and they meet as often as once a week to discuss the stock market or other investment vehicles. The group approach of an investment club provides the beginner with a supportive environment in which to discuss market segments, strategies, and specific stocks with others who know a bit more than you do. To find a club, or to start one of your own, contact the National Association of Investment Clubs, in Washington, D.C.

You might also want to find out if there are investment plans available through the fringe benefit package where you work. Corporations such as IBM, Xerox, and Hilton have spent enormous amounts of time and energy putting together seductive benefit packages to entice their employees to stay with them. These packages often include investment plans, which are an excellent place for a beginning investor to start, since they're typically among the most solid arrangements available (for the simple reason that corporations don't want their employees worrying about risky financial dealings). Some companies offer their own stock to employees at lower-than-market prices, as well as presenting other plans with money market funds at varying degrees of risk.

There are also a number of books that will quickly provide you with background information on the market. While reading is a more passive exercise than the others I have mentioned, it can be worthwhile—as long as it is followed by some sort of action.

The following are tops on my list of primers for the beginning stock market investor:

The Battle for Investment Survival
   by Gerald Loeb
How to Buy Stocks by Louis Engel

On basic investing, try the following:

The Only Investment Guide You'll Ever Need
   by Andrew Tobias
How to Survive on $50,000 to $150,000 a Year
   by Stanley J. Cohen and Robert Wool

The Joy of Money by Paula Nelson

Situation: You want to start investing in real estate.

Suggested Action: The fastest way to learn about real estate is to become a member of an investment team. By going in with two or three other people, you cushion the potential risks and create a safer learning environment. In addition, you have an opportunity to learn from and with each other. It's an approach that's used by sophisticated investors as well as novices, and you can follow their successful lead if you keep a few pointers in mind.

Be sure to have a written contract covering the following items: specifications and percentages of ownership of each investor, methods for acquiring additional properties, procedures for handling a withdrawal from the team by one or more investors (specifically that a "right of first refusal" be written into the contract so the remaining members won't end up with a surprise partner), circumstances under which the property can be sold, and individual responsibilities of each investor—who will pay the taxes, who will look after the repairs, and who will collect rents if it's an income property.

It's a good idea, too, to make certain that one partner is in a stronger financial position than the others to guard against a run of bad luck that could force you into foreclosure for missing a single payment.

While team investing might not give you enormous returns on your investment, the potential for loss isn't great, either.

For background reading, try any of Albert J. Lowry's books or *Creating Wealth* by Robert G. Allen.

Situation: You have an idea, product, company, or service you'd like to take to the marketplace.

Suggested Actions: First, write up a business plan. (See the Appendix.) It can be fast and rough, just as long as you get the basic concepts and ideas down. Then you can go back and polish it up.

Second, run an ad in *The Wall Street Journal* for backers, distribution outlets, associates, venture capitalists to invest in your idea, or whatever.

Third, practice the concept of "show up and show off," which is precisely what I did many years ago when I took the proposal for my first book to the American Booksellers Association convention and walked the convention until I lined up a publisher. No matter what idea, product, or service you have in mind, there is probably a trade show or convention that deals with that area. Take your idea to those in the field and get their reaction. You might also line up backers, distributors, and outlets at the same time.

Situation: You have an invention you'd like to market.

Suggested Actions: As I described in Chapter 3, Spot It/Test It/Package It, you need to develop a prototype, do a production-cost analysis, and then take your prototype to the market to see if there is a demand for the product at the price you want to sell it for.

Situation: You need backers for your venture.

Suggested Actions: First, reread Chapter 5, NCR: No Cash Required. Second, write up a business plan. Third, set up meetings with money sources and present your plan. You can also place an ad in

The Wall Street Journal soliciting investors, and you can ask your banker to introduce you to venture capitalists in your area.

Matching up projects and investors is not an overnight project. You're looking for a match between one specific interest and another, which is difficult to do even when you're dealing with venture capitalists. But with persistence and a plan of action, it can be done.

Situation: You want to collect money that is owed to you.

Suggested Actions: Part of the "getting rich" process is the "getting richer" process—and that might involve collecting money that is owed to you but is not being repaid as agreed.

If you're owed money that you don't seem to be able to collect, you have several choices. You can simply shrug your shoulders and categorize the situation as an impossible collection, which means that it becomes a tax write-off. Or you can bring in an outside party, such as a collection agency, an attorney, or an arbitrator to handle the situation.

Situation: You aren't sure where to invest.

Suggested Actions: In this book you've seen how to develop your vision and direct your attention to the many potential areas of investment available to you. If you want to start making investments but aren't sure which field to go into, start by taking your own personal economic/investment inventory, using the broad categories outlined in Chapter 2, Economic Orbit of Opportunity. It's through the inventory process that you will begin to recognize the investment areas with the greatest potential for you.

Remember, it's more important for you to invest in things you *know about, enjoy,* and have an *affinity for* than to follow what the latest economic guru is touting as the hot new investment fad. There will always be fads in investing, just as there are in nearly every other area of life, but you stand a better chance of building a strong, stable portfolio if you stick to things you know and understand.

Situation: You are starting to get concerned about your financial security after retirement.

Suggested Actions: It's never too early to start preparing for your retirement years. You can take instant action by automating the process of saving by setting a payroll deduction plan into motion where you work. You can set up an annuity program or you can structure a specific retirement investment.

For example, I recently chatted with a banker in Birmingham, Alabama, who is investing in a real estate venture that won't produce any positive cash flow for at least ten years. He told me that he doesn't need the cash now—in fact it would place him in a less advantageous tax bracket—but he's figuring his eventual retirement budget with the delayed income in mind. You can check out similar possibilities in your area.

As these scenarios have demonstrated, the possibility for instant action is right there in front of you, no matter what your economic situation might be or which financial scenario you want to set in motion. You are the only one who can initiate this instant action, but once you decide to take that step, you'll begin to see just how easy—and profitable—action can be.

What I wanted to do most in this book was to open your eyes to the nearly limitless moneymaking opportunities all around you—many within your reach this very moment.

These principles are designed to give you a powerful arsenal of insight into the moneymaking process—the same insight shared by the most successful women and men in the world. You will enjoy a new understanding of the money game, its real workings, its boundless possibilities and options for your personal success.

Use my principles. Practice them. Study them. Discuss them. As you do, you will find yourself beginning a new and valuable adventure toward freeing your profit potential in all areas of your life.

You will learn too that making money is fun, as I hope I have shown on these pages. But it is much more than that. By becoming financially aware and involved, you will find the key not only to security and independence, but to your success as a mature human being. It is your right to take control of your financial future, but you will learn that it is a delight, too. Creatively pursued, the money game is the most exciting game of all! Come join those of us who've found that financial awareness has brought a sound and rewarding life-style. We did it, and so can you. Now go to it!

I have one request of you. Just as I ask my lecture and seminar friends to keep me informed about how they have profited from my principles, I am asking you for your reactions too. Write and tell me how the principles worked for you. This book is a two-way conversation, a talk between us. Now, I want to hear from you. Write to me at:

> The Money Forum
> 712 Wilshire Blvd.
> Suite 1014
> Santa Monica, CA 90401

The Business Plan

Your goal should be to write a business plan that's solid, that sells, and that sizzles, because a plan that meets these criteria will be your most valuable asset in getting the money you need. In fact, it will become your primary selling tool for raising cash—whether you're going after $50,000 or $50,000,000. It will also provide you and your associates with the assurance you need that your company is financially viable, with a strong profit potential.

I always suggest that the key person(s) in the venture should prepare the first draft of the Business Plan because that person is the most intimately involved in the operation and therefore has the most insight and enthusiasm. You can always have someone else polish the grammar and punctuation later, but your initial goal should be to spell out the Who, What, Where, Why, and How much of your existing or proposed company.

You can make the plan as detailed as you wish. Some run 100 pages or more, but most of the plans I'm involved with are about twenty pages long. My advice is to make the document succinct but complete. Many people have their plan bound in a quality binder. I recommend that approach because it lets potential investors know that you mean business and that you take your project seriously.

The first page should be a title page listing the name of the company, the date, and a statement that the plan is a confidential document not to be duplicated or passed on to others without permission.

The second page should be a table of contents that looks something like this:

    Purpose or Summary
    The Company's Business or Product Line
    Strategy and Product Line
    Marketing
    Competition
    Creative Personnel
    Production
    Financing Requirements
    Management
    Advisory Board
    Expansion Plans
    Financial Forecasts:
      Earnings Forecasts
      Cash Forecasts
      Balance Sheet Forecast
      Source and Application of Funds Forecast

Don't let this table of contents intimidate you. In the next few pages I'll give you some hints on what information to include under each heading.

Purpose or Summary: Write one paragraph that clearly states what you're trying to accomplish. For example:

> To obtain initial capitalization or to organize a company that will manufacture state-of-the-art audio and visual products and services to be marketed to national and international audio and visual markets.

This portion of the Business Plan will quickly let potential investors know if yours is a product or service that's of interest to them.

The Company's Business or Product Line: Discuss the products and/or services you'll be providing in more specific terms. For example, if your business plan is for a video dating service, you might write that your business is the taping and computer matching of like-minded adults in major metropolitan areas throughout the country, adding that it's the company's objective to become the leading video dating service in the country.

A straightforward statement will usually find a winning response from the reader.

Strategy and Product Line: This section should cover your positioning in the marketplace, describe what's unique about your product or service, and how it will fill a gap in the particular market you're aiming at.

Marketing: Describe how you're going to deliver your product or service to the marketplace. Explain the distribution system you'll use, and provide any other information that will give the investor the feeling that you've worked out all the important details. For example, you might write that you're going to use existing dealer/distributor networks in combination with direct-mail sales, or that you're planning to attend various conventions to line up distributors. Always fill in the names of key individuals who'll play a pivotal role in the marketing function.

Competition: This section should reflect your solid knowledge of the market, including information about who your competitors will be and how you plan to position yourself in relation to them. If, for example, you're intending to open a weight-reduction gym and fail to mention in your business plan that your competitor will be a large franchise of the same type in the same neighborhood, you'd be revealing a serious lack of business sense.

Creative People—Engineers, Designers, Writers, Etc.: Virtually every business has a creative end that's involved in conceptualizing new ideas for products and/or services. In this section of your plan, name the individuals in your operation who fill this function and provide details about their background, accomplishments, and any awards they may have received or special claims to fame. Since the purpose of your business plan is to let potential investors know why you're different from—and more worthy than—others who might

190

also be seeking them as investors, you shouldn't be modest about the superiority of your creative staff.

Production: This is the place to wax poetic about your business's production process.

Financing: State exactly how much money you need and how much ownership in your company you're willing to give up for that money. For example, you might write:

> To accomplish our stated goals, we require $250,000 over the coming 12-month period commencing January 1. In consideration of the $250,000, we are prepared to offer you 40 percent of the company.

Investors reading that statement would know exactly what the stakes of the deal are before they sit down at the bargaining table. They might not go for your offer, but at least you will be sure that you have presented it in a manner they can evaluate and react to.

Management: This is where you roll out the big ammunition. You should include crisp but impressive biographies of each member of the organization, including those you plan to hire after you secure funding. (Including information about those who are not yet on board indicates foresight as well as smart packaging. It shows that you're already planning for the future, which is attractive to potential investors.)

Advisory Board: This is the section of the business plan where you sweeten the package and increase

191

the attractiveness of your proposal to the investor. Members of the Advisory Board should be the smartest, most respected people you know in your industry, people who are willing to serve on your board because they believe in you and what you're doing. For example, if you're a recent graduate of a university school of business management, and your business plan is for a consulting firm, you might ask a former professor with a particularly strong reputation in the field to serve on your Advisory Board. If you're an accountant with many customers in the legal field, you could ask a client who's a prominent attorney to serve on your board.

About the Author

Known to millions from her appearances on NBC's *Today Show* and on *Hour Magazine,* Paula Nelson cofounded three electronics companies before the age of thirty. Her best-selling book *the Joy of Money,* published in 1976, is now in its twelfth printing. Her second book, *Where to Get Money for Everything,* was published in 1982. Her by-line has appeared in *Newsweek, Saturday Evening Post, McCall's,* and *Self.* She lectures nationally to Fortune 500 companies, financial institutions, and small-business groups and associations. She serves on the board of two California corporations and is president of The Money Forum, a company devoted to financial education through seminars and a monthly newsletter.